# A Licence To Live

## Ron Barnes

# Scenes from a post-war working life in Hackney

Copyright © 1974 Ron Barnes
Reprinted 1975

Published by Hackney Workers' Educational Association and
Hackney Libraries Committee. Distributed by Centerprise
136/138 Kingsland High Street  E8. 01-254 9632/5. Printed by
Expression Printers Ltd  5 Kingsbury Road  London N1 4AZ

ISBN 0 903738 08 2

*dedicated to my Father*

# Introduction

What has prompted me to write this book, I don't know. I was always rather poor at all subjects at school, due to having considerable time off with asthma. My arithmetic and spelling were, and still are, very bad. But being in my late thirties I have experienced a complete new outlook on life. Since a child, living in the East End of London, life has always seemed a puzzle to me. I suppose I am not alone in this. But I think the reason I have written this is that all my experiences, good and bad, seem to have built up inside, and this is one way of giving vent to my feelings about life in general.

But what has made me aware of the conditions of life, and what life and survival are all about, and how education is so important to people, is my reading of the *Morning Star*, and although I don't agree with all it says, it does give one what you call news, important news. This paper has caused me to become an avid reader also. At one time I was oblivious of day to day events and current affairs, but not so today.

Another reason why I decided to write this is because I have never kept a diary. I don't think many people in the working class in Hackney keep diaries either. Yet haven't you ever wondered what life was like for 'ordinary' people centuries ago? Not only people in general, but perhaps your ancestors, the people that you yourself have descended from. Haven't you ever wished that you could get a glimpse into the lives of your past relatives, and to take yourself back to those past times, and get the feel of just what people were like then, their way of life, their pleasures, joys, disappointments, fears, and most important of all, their personal deep feelings and their impression of the world they lived in.

Well I had such a desire myself. Then I got to thinking: Well the aristocracy are able to trace back their ancestors, generation after generation, why shouldn't ordinary people be able to do the same? And so with these thoughts in my mind, I decided to write the accounts that you find in this book. I am also getting together as many old photographs as possible of all my relatives — wedding photos, holiday snaps, parties and special events that have taken place — and of course all other material that I can get my hands on, like driving licences, rent rebate forms or cuttings from newspapers that dealt with my family or friends. I would want to leave some time over, to satisfy my one over-ruling desire to become a reasonably good artist.

I am very grateful to Centerprise and the Hackney Workers' Educational Association, who started this project on Hackney history and encouraging people to write about their lives. My book may not be a work of art, and void of intellectual phrases; it may have a touch of self-pity about it, but there it is. To me this has been a great achievement, a thing that some years ago I would never have dreamed of doing. I would like to thank sincerely, Ken Worpole who encouraged me in this project of writing, Neil Martinson who did all the designing on the book, and Mick Hugo who did the drawings for the cover.

It is certain that there are thousands of people in Hackney who can write, but have never tried it. When I have spoken to people about writing they've always said, 'What me? I could never write anything, I haven't the words or the patience for it.' Most people seem to be under the impression that they have to have a top class education before they can write anything. Nothing could be further from the truth. With the little experience I have had, I would like to say to would-be writers this: Just sit down and write. It may be a story, part of your autobiography, or a poem; just write it as it comes and put in your change of words later. The manuscript I took into Centerprise was quite a mess: my spelling was atrocious, not a clue about where to put paragraphs, punctuation marks were non-existent except for a few commas and full stops. I just wrote it down as it came into my mind, and talked about ordering it into shape with Ken and Neil at Centerprise.

One thing I am sure of is that there is a story in every one of us which will come out if we give it a chance to. If you enjoy this story I hope it will encourage you to write your own; if you don't enjoy it then at least it will be a guide to you on how not to write your story. So by writing you not only give other people a certain amount of pleasure, but you also benefit yourself. And certainly we owe it to ourselves to develop our talents, talents which are there lying inside every one of us. If we grasp the opportunities that we now have there is no telling just what we people in Hackney could achieve. I sincerely hope that you will enjoy reading this book, and I hope that it will encourage you to write something of your own.


Ron Barnes
14 January 1974

# 1

The 1939-45 war had begun. My mother and father were making for Bury St. Edmunds in Norfolk. My father had not been fit enough for the army. My father's mother was to meet us down there. She had about ten children in all, my father being the eldest boy. My grandmother was a real Cockney in her ways and mannerisms. She was about four feet, ten inches tall, round and dumpy all over. She must have weighed twelve stone or more and as she walked along she seemed to roll from side to side and it made one feel that she would overbalance any minute – and this she did do on numerous occasions, especially after a session in the 'White Hart' along the Bethnal Green Road.

She never started drinking until she was about forty. This I found out from my grandmother on my mother's side. My parents had lived in the same street, Poyser Street, which had two ends, one being the posh end and the other being the rough end. My two grandmothers lived at the posh end in their younger days, and from what I can gather everything between them was O.K.

My dad's parents seemed to manage all right, and were considered lucky. The 'old man', as my nan called her husband, worked for Carter Pattersons for over forty years. But when their children numbered three, the landlady told the family that they must go. The only available place in the street that was large enough for them was down the rough end, and this was the beginning of her drinking habit.

The women used to sit in the pub shelling peas. Most of them were costermongers' wives, and, much as gran disliked beer at first, they managed to get her on it. Although my father never said anything to me, I think he was heart-broken to see the change in his mother after forming the habit of drink.

After he got married, he would hardly ever go to see her: he would say, 'Pubs! They ought to close the lot of them down. They cause more trouble than enough!' I could quite understand his feelings. My grandfather would come home and find her out, and the dinner not cooked, and this would lead to a row, and sometimes a fight. What a lesson this is on human nature and the effects of the environment. She did not have to move to another street, not even another district, but just down the road lay unhappiness, fighting, dirt, drunkenness and poverty, sickness and all kinds of nervous conditions.

Yet despite the hardships of those days, my grandmother had a great personality. I didn't used to see her much, but I can never remember seeing her miserable: she was always jolly, no matter what. She had a round chubby face, with rosy red cheeks and two sparkling pale blue eyes which seemed to be smiling all the time. My gran on my mother's side, Granny Gulliss, had often told me how attractive Gran Barnes used to be. Her once shiny black hair was now a beautiful silver, with a most unusual sparkle in it. How a woman living the hard life of those days can come through with such an appearance and personality I shall never know.

Well we finally made it to Hill House, Bury St. Edmunds. I believe this place was an old mansion belonging to some Lord or Squire in the old days. The front did not have a very welcoming look and reminded me of some ancient house that you'd be likely to see in a horror film. The hall was stone-tiled and there were these old fashioned bells hanging round the wall to summon the servants with. As you pulled a lever in one part of the house it set them ringing. These bells were functioning quite well when we arrived, but after the kids had finished playing with them and had driven everybody crazy with the continuous ringing, these bells could stand no more and gave up the ghost, much to the adults' satisfaction. It was a big, cold house and every floor was made of stone. In the winter it was freezing, and we could hardly afford to keep a fire going in the big kitchen, which was the smallest room in the house and the warmest. A fire in the other rooms was out of the question, certainly while my father was unable to get work.

This state of affairs led to the gradual disappearance of the old barn at the back of the house. Bit by bit it gradually diminished until there was nothing left. It began with one plank, my mother saying to my father, 'Oh, Bill, don't pull any more down or we will get chucked out.' And my father replying, 'Well if we get no heating they'll have to carry us out'. I think this was one of the things that helped bring on my asthma. Anyway, the next day it was two planks, then three, then four. When the demolition work reached this advanced stage, the kids were only too willing to help Dad finally bring it all to the ground. That old barn was a godsend to us all that first winter.

When the billeting officer came, the dismantling was in its early stages. The officer was a big, fat, healthy-looking man. He wore a black overcoat with his large paunch trying to burst out of it. His fat face possessed an unnaturally pointed nose, a nose so thin that it did not seem to match the face. His eyes were black and beady-looking.

'This will never do,' he said. And each time he called, the barn had reached a further stage of disintegration. My mother began to get really worried about it. My father said to her,

'Well, what do they expect, sending us to a place like this out in no-mans-land, and no work. And if there were work, how would we get coal out here in this god-forsaken place?'

When the billeting officer called the next time, he saw that the shed was almost gone. He was really mad.

'Mr Barnes,' he said to my father. 'If any more of that shed is taken down the next time I call, you will have to leave these premises and you will find yourself facing a court charge. Now, please, no more.'

My father was mad. 'And if my kid catches pneumonia because there's no fuel, you might find yourself in trouble too, if this weather continues. I tell you now, that shed is coming down, unless you do something to help us, which, after all, is what you're supposed to be for, instead of threatening us with eviction and police courts. Good day!'

The officer walked out fuming.

Two or three days later the billeting officer called again. My mother saw him coming down the path and she was frantic with worry. There was a bang on the door. 'I'll see to him,' said my dad.

'Good morning, Mr Barnes.'

'You're entitled to your opinion,' said dad.

'I have come to inform you . . . ' said the officer.

My mother stopped what she was doing and waited for the worst.

'I have come to inform you that later in the day there will be a supply of coal delivered here. I don't know how much there will be — as you know, everything is so short at the moment, and I cannot promise that there will be more — but it will be something to be going on with.'

'Het, make the man a cup of tea,' said my father.

Well the coal arrived. It wasn't much, like the officer said, but it was something to go on with. The trouble was that we would get sweating hot in the kitchen, and when we went into the bedrooms, it was like a fridge. I would lay awake for hours before getting warm and finally dropping off to sleep.

For some reason or other we eventually left Hill House, but just before that my grandmother had to leave for other accommodation in Bury St. Edmunds. Of course we went with her to find the new place. We had a terrible job to find it, and by the time we arrived it was pitch black. It was in the winter and snowing and we had to cut across ploughed fields to get to the house. Being only nine years old, I was terrified, and, freezing cold, we laboured our way through the snow, with our bundles of small belongings. We had almost given up trying to find the house, and if it had not have been so dark we would have gone back to Hill House.

'There it is, over there!' cried my father suddenly. Over there was right. It was about half a mile over there with a fence running across the field to be scaled by mum, dad, the children and gran. The thoughts of a warm fire and something to eat spurred us on. We finally got to the fence when suddenly we heard a cry from out of the darkness. 'Whoooer! Whoooer!' We looked back and could see nothing. We began to walk back in the direction of the cry and then we saw something white on the ground: it was the bottom end of gran. She had fallen into a ditch. Everybody else had been lucky to avoid it, unknowingly, because the snow had hidden it, but poor gran had found it and there she was, upside down. The bundle she had been carrying was now covering her face, and she lay in the ditch, her legs up in the air and her pantaloons waving in the breeze. We then had to summon all hands to hoist her out of the ditch, as she was no light weight, going about fourteen stone or so. Being short and dumpy did not make our task any easier. But after many grunts and groans, gran was finally rescued.

It had taken a lot out of us by this time, but the worst was yet to come, for we had to scale the fence ahead, and what a job that would be with gran.

We managed to get over the fence, after much straining and per- severence, and we were now looking forward to that big fire and a cup of tea. We made our way towards the big, black door, on that freezing night, the wind blowing snow at us from all directions. My father knocked on the door. We waited and waited. It seemed the door would never open. We then heard a scraping along the floor, inside the house, with the blackness all around us and the freezing cold. I was terrified. The door slowly came open, and as we looked we could see nothing but blackness. There was a voice coming from the floor saying,

'Hello, who is it? What can I do for you?'

We looked down and there on the floor was a lamp burning, and something moved.

After our eyes became accustomed to the light we could see the face of an old lady, sort of squatting on the floor.

'I was told that you had a bit of room for some evacuees,' said gran.

The deathly white face looked over the lamp at us. She had a well-worn scarf around her head, but you could see by some of the hair around the edge of the scarf that she was very grey, her face thin, her eyes sunken. She was clearly a woman in ill-health.

'Well, you had better come in.'

I was stricken with fear at those words. I felt like running for safety, but behind was complete blackness. I was trapped. She turned her back on us and we followed her in. She crawled along the floor pushing the lamp in front of her as she went.

'I'm sorry there's no fire for you,' she said. 'But there's some wood in the box there if you would like to light it.'

My father opened the box, took out the sticks and began to light the fire.

'I don't suppose we could have a cup of tea, gal, could we?'

'Yes,' the old lady answered, 'help yourself.'

Gran didn't need any second telling. On went the kettle, and tea was up in no time. All this was going on with only the light of the old lady's oil lamp. Behind us and around us were deep, long shadows, like monsters ready to pounce any minute.

The room was about ten feet long and six feet wide. It contained one table, a wooden armchair, one upright wooden chair and a bed in the corner. The old lady was in bed when we called, therefore the bed was in complete disarray. It seemed as though someone was still laying in the bed, but this was because of the way the covers were ruffled up.

This gruesome experience as a child will always be in my mind. This poor old lady crawling about the floor, living alone deep in the country. Being a child, surrounded by darkness, with the cold weather and the poverty of this house: all these things helped to make me terrified of this harmless old lady.

And yet poverty is frightening, and even more so when you are trying to escape from its terrible jaws. You go to work and save ten pounds and you think you have beaten poverty. You become sick and find that within a week poverty is the victor. After months of toil, going to work unfit to keep the monster at bay, within a week poverty is the winner, and as the weeks go by the teeth bite ever deeper. The same as I felt in that house in the darkness: you turn to run only to meet more darkness.

Gran decided that this place would not be suitable for the family , so she announced that we should go back to Hill House. Immediately. It was no use arguing with gran: what she said went. So we had to trek back again three miles to Hill House, back again over the fence and keeping close to gran to see that she didn't go down another ditch.

Why we made that trip to that old house on that night I don't know. It could have been that we were looking for somewhere more comfortable, but as big and cold as Hill House was, it was better than the place we had just visited.

A few days after this trip, gran announced,

'I'm going to make you kids a nice suet pud.'

This caused the kids to go mad with delight. We had just come home from school and after we had our bread and jam we usually went out to play in the graveyard behind the house. But not tonight. Each one was going to make sure that he not only got a bit of this promised pudding, but that his share was equal to everybody else's. All of us waited in the kitchen, a couple sitting on the stone floor by the fire playing with some string, making patterns with it, one of the girls slumped in an old, torn armchair reading the remains of an old comic, myself and Johnny, my uncle, only a year and a half older than myself, just standing together a yard or two from the boiling pot, glancing at gran now and again, hoping to see her get up and announce the meal was ready to be served.

The massive pot began to boil over. Gran had dozed off. 'Gran! Gran!' came the chorus from the kids. 'It's on the boil! It's on the boil!' Gran wakes with a start.

'Cor blimey, you'd think the house was alight! What's the matter – you all bleedin' starving or something?' She then gets up from her high-backed wooden chair, makes her way slowly to the bubbling potful of pudding, slowly turns the gas down and says,

'It isn't done yet.'

A groan of despair comes from the kids, as she makes her way back to the armchair.

'How long then, mum,?' says John.

'Oh, about ten minutes.'

The kids look at each other and smile.

At last gran was getting the pudding pot off the gas. It was more like a small bath than a pot, judging by her efforts. I thought 'this must be some suet pudding'. Her small, fat figure turned away from the cooker and clutching the pot with both hands, by a handle each side, she steadily made her towards the table at the far side of the kitchen, steam seeping through the rim of the lid as she went. The children followed behind in single file, the eldest in front and the youngest at the back. It was as though the nursery rhyme, 'The Little Old Lady Who Lived in a Shoe' was brought to life.

The bottom of the pot was now resting on gran's belly and she heaved it on to the table. As she removed the lid, a vast area of the kitchen was filled with steam. She then pushed a long bar of metal through the knot she had tied in the cloth which held the pudding and tried to hoist it out. But the pudding proved much too heavy.

'Here, Bill!' she cried to my father. 'Gi' us an 'and to git this 'ere thing out!'

He came promptly to the rescue. As the pudding came in full view of the potential consumers, their eyes opened wide with surprise or perhaps fear. For to me this enormous pudding had the appearance of a great steaming monster which was being balanced on the end of a great iron bar by dad, who by now was red and sweating with the efforts of trying to dislodge the pudding from the pot.

At last the children had got what they had been waiting for: suet pudding with jam!

For reasons unknown, my parents left Hill House and we found ourselves on a farmhouse in Norfolk. By moving to this place, I felt completely cut off. There were no children and I used to amuse myself in the fields. Surprisingly, there were no horses or cows in the fields. The farmer must have kept them in their sheds most of the time, because I could never remember any.

At one time I found some long stems to use as hurdles to jump over. I was promptly stopped by Uncle Ernie the farmer. It turned out that these stems were rhubarb, and where I had been unable to clear them, at every jump they had been broken.

Uncle Ernie was about forty-five, and Grannie Camel, his mother, was about seventy. The house was situated in a part of no-mans-land.

There was absolutely nothing for me to do after school, summer or winter. Of an evening we would sit round the fire in the house with one oil lamp burning on the table. Grannie Camel would be sitting in a wooden armchair dozing off to sleep, clutching a small bundle, which I think was her life's savings. Every night, before she settled in her armchair, she would go upstairs and get her bundle. There was an accumulator wireless set on the table. This was our only entertainment. Uncle Earnie would be sitting in an upright chair, gripping his stomach and groaning with indigestion. I would be sitting in an old armchair with a black cat. He was my only companion at theat farm and I can't even remember his name.

For some reason or other, we left Grannie Camel's and I then found myself back in London amongst the bombing, which increased my nervousness. My father stayed in the country working at an ammunition factory, while my mother and I came home.

We would go to bed at night, knowing that we would soon have to get up when the sirens sounded, about one or two in the morning. I would awake terrified, snatched out of my bed by someone, and wrapped in a thick blanket. I would be taken down the stairs into the shelter adjacent to the flats. There was about six of us altogether, as far as I can remember. There was my mother, gran, two aunts and Uncle George, my gran's brother. As we came down the stairs, we heard a bomb whistling down. It sounded as though it was right on top of us. A few seconds after that, there was a bang of such enormity that it would be impossible to describe to anyone who has never heard a bomb drop. Being only about ten or eleven, I was truly horrified and bewildered. I wanted to cry but couldn't. I wanted to scream but something seemed to be stopping me — some invisible force.

We finally made it to the shelter; the sight and smell I then encountered has stuck in my mind ever since. As I write this I can smell the strong carbolic that was sprinkled on the floors, mingling with the smell of sweat from the people's beds, who slept down the shelter every night, the smell of urine from the children's bunks, who were, like myself, in the habit of wetting their beds. The bunks were lined along the wall, three high, at one end of the long shelter. Those who couldn't sleep, or who could not be accommodated on the bunks, had to sleep on the floor, which was made of concrete. The walls were bare brick, the lighting almost nil. There were old people and mothers with their young children sleeping on this hard, cold floor. I wonder what the health of those young children is like now?

Usually, when we had to stay down the shelter all night, we would play cards and even at my young age I would join in. But if my Uncle George walked in, after a session at The Wheatsheaf in Windas Road, he would break into song. This would cause a few others to join in. I had a ukelele, which I used to strum and away we used to go. We would sing songs like, 'The White Cliffs of Dover', 'Bless them all', 'Pack up your troubles', 'Ma, he's making eyes at me', 'When the lights go on again' and many more. This used to cheer us up no end, so that we wouldn't even notice the dull lighting and the red brick wall.

During the war, there was a complaint going around called scabies. This complaint was mostly amongst the working class, who used to sleep down the shelters. My aunt and her children who came to live next door used to come in to us of a night for company. We were all infested with the scabies, otherwise known as 'the itch'. It was of a night that the fun would start. It only wanted one of us kids to scratch his nose with his little finger and someone else would start. Eventually we were all scratching like a load of monkeys.

As soon as my mother and my aunt saw this scratching competition in progress, out would come the sulphur bath and in we would go. This would be the only thing to bring the scratching to an end.

Someone in the family became poetical about the affair and composed this song, sung to the tune of 'Bless them all'. This is another example of the cockney sense of humour, even in poverty and sickness.

*I know of a house where they've all got the itch,*
*Upstairs and downstairs the same,*
*Scratching in this room and scratching in that,*
*Scratching their arm-holes and scratching their backs.*

*And if you should see them you would laugh,*
*When they're taking a nice sulphur bath,*
*What more could they do with the old itchy coo,*
*Have a scratch, have a scratch, have a scratch.*

*And they say it is nice to be rich,*
*But all they have got is the itch,*
*They dream of the day when the itch goes away,*
*And they won't have to scratch, have to scratch.*

After about nine months, we left gran's and went to the country again and came back just before the end of the war. We came back to live in Stoke Newington. The house contained two families, both Jewish. There was an old lady named Mrs Alex, who was called Boober, and her husband who was called Mr Alex. Their daughter, Hetty, lived downstairs with her husband and two sons. They were marvellous people. We lived at the top of the house. My father was unemployed for a long time after the war, and things were very bad for us. I used to wear my shoes out so quickly that my father could not keep up with the mending of my shoes. He had plenty of time to do them but lacked the money to buy the leather. Whether one could apply for clothing at the Assistance Board or not, I don't know, but I cannot remember ever getting any. When it was wet my feet would get soaked and I would have to sit in school all day, my socks drying on my feet.

When my dad was working for George Ewer, at the end of the war, he had to carry fish in a covered waggon. Sometimes, or should I say quite often, I would bunk off school and wait for him to come out of his garage and wave him down.

'Why ain't you at school?' he would ask.

'Well I want to come with you, dad. You know I hate school.'

'All right, jump up, but don't let your mother know.'

I used to like those days out, especially when he had to go out into the country, and on the way back he would let me collect some chestnuts. What I didn't like though was the smell of the fish and the petrol mingling together. I don't know how my dad could have done this job really, but he used to say,

'Well, I get more money for this, than I would carting other goods.'

But in the summer it was shocking, the bluebottles would follow him all the way home. He smelt terrible. Mr Alex who lived downstairs would spray the passage with some disinfectant every night after my father had come in. This job got my father going on the sale of empty boxes, just another of his attempts at making his fortune.

Almost every commodity on the market was rationed during the war, and where you felt it most was on clothing and food. Our parents had gone through very hard times during the thirties; so bad were those times that when people are talking about that period today, they refer to them as 'the hungry thirties'. If the thirties were hungry, then the first part of the forties were even hungrier.

Each family was allowed something like two ounces of butter per person per week; a quarter pound of sugar, and one egg, although I can never remember seeing one of these throughout the war. So the people found life even harder. Beforehand, there was unemployment on a vast scale, and they had to eke out on what little money they could earn, steal or borrow. But now it wasn't only the money problem they had, but the rationing as well. Consequently, if they had the money they had no coupons, and if they had the coupons they had no money. To get over this problem of money they would sell their coupons, although this practice was illegal, and when they had money and no coupons then they would buy from someone else, and that's how it went on.

A government slogan came out during this time entreating people to: 'Make do and mend'. Someone somewhere must have been well out of touch, for many of the working people had done nothing else all their lives. Their ingenuity was unsurpassed as far as that was concerned. An old pair of socks would become a pair of mittens; the limp wool of an old pullover would find itself skilfully changed into a scarf, or pixie. This was a sort of scarf sewn in such a way as to make a hat of it as well as a scarf.

The children were allowed about two ounces of sweets a week. If you were greedy and scoffed the lot by Wednesday, then you had to wait until the following week for your next lot, or you could go into your local sweetshop with your most sorrowful look and say, 'Please, Mr King, mummy said (you mustn't forget the mummy said bit for he might think you had nicked the ration book out of her bag) would you please let me have some sweets off of next week's rations?' If he was a man with any feeling for kids he would risk it and chance getting a fine. But in the shop I used to go to you had to be careful because sometimes there would be a policeman standing in the shop. If you had a lot of adults in your family it wasn't too bad, because they would give up their coupons to the children, and sometimes the kids would even have a Sunday trip round to all the aunts and uncles to see if there were any coupons going. In acquiring the coupons they then had to find ways and means of getting the money. The kids who couldn't get the coupons would have to settle for a halfpenny carrot or apple. But those who could take it would sometimes buy two ounces of cough sweets from the chemist — these weren't rationed — and after these had been in your mouth a few seconds it felt as though they had burnt a hole through your tongue, they were that hot. All children had to have their feet measured every so often to assess how many coupons they were entitled to for footwear. The trick was: when the measurer took the width of your foot you would press down as hard as you could to make your foot wider. In this way you could possibly gain a few extra coupons.

The black market was rampant: to the racketeers this war was a godsend. They would charge two or three times the normal price for anything they obtained for a person. There are people today who have the war to thank for the wealth that they are enjoying now. When the war ended they cried their eyes out.

And many others cried with joy at seeing their sons and daughters safely back home. There were street parties everywhere: they brought out their furniture, tables chairs, settees and pianos. I was one of the musicians down one of these streets; it went on all day and night. The feeling among the people was touching indeed: a mother dancing with her soldier son, looking at him with tears in her eyes thinking, I shouldn't wonder, how lucky she was to have him back, and not only that, but to have him back in one piece.

Wives sitting with their husbands, ever so closely, the children all round their soldier daddy, and you may spot one or two mothers trying to coax a child to let this man hold them. For some of these children had still been in their mother's womb when their fathers had gone to war. The concern and love and sympathy these people showed to each other, especially to those who had lost a loved one, would be unbelievable today. It's a pity this feeling had to quickly fizzle out when the era of the rat race began.

# 2

The first signs of asthma came on after the war, when I was
about twelve. But years before this I was always sniffing and caught
colds rather quickly. I was playing in the street, running about like
children do, when suddenly I could not get my breath. I had to sit
down for a while until I felt better. This was the first starting of it.
Just after this I was put into the top class. I was never happy at
school, due to bad attendance. Consequently I lost out on lessons.
I could not grasp what they were trying to teach me. In fact I
became rather afraid of going to school, lest I made a fool of myself
during lessons when teacher would start asking questions on a
subject I knew nothing about. Somehow I was able to conceal my
ignorance, by keeping quiet and not mixing too much with the
other kids.

I was not a very bright child at school, but the lesson I used to
love was Art. The rest of the subjects were most obscure. This was
because I had much time off school due to asthma. The teachers
didn't really get to know just what I could or could not do. They
did not know that I was keen on music and art, who can tell who
is really to blame?

I was never able to become attached to any one boy, and make
a friend of him, and I have always been like this all through my life.
What I do love are music and art, talents which I have never been
able to develop, the first reason being that these two interests were
never discovered by the school, and secondly, that my parents knew
that I had these interests, but for some reason never encouraged
them, probably due to the cares they had from living day to day.

Also there were no other children in my neighbourhood who
had any interest in art or music. Or were there, but they were stifled
just like me? When I was about twelve I loved the piano and the
accordian, and made up my mind that I would have both when I

started to work. The first thing I did as soon as I started work was to go to a music teacher of the accordian. I had already started to play the piano after a style. My grandmother had a piano which I played at every opportunity.

When I arrived at the music teacher's house, she asked me if I had an accordian. I told her I hadn't.

'Well, it's no good having lessons without possessing an instrument,' she said.

At these words I felt beaten, and I think she noticed this, for she then said to me,

'I have an accordian that you could buy, if you like. I'll go and get it.'

When I saw this beautiful instrument I fell in love with it straight away. It was a forty-eight base, rose mother of pearl.

'Oh, it's a beauty,' I said.

She then played a tune on it, and it sounded even better than it looked. If only I could play like that, I thought.

'Well,' she said. 'If you like it, it's only twenty pounds.'

This was a great deal of money to me at that time, earning about three pounds, ten shillings a week. When I told here that I didn't have the sort of money, she agreed to let me pay so much a week, but I had to leave the accordian with her until it was paid up.

I broke myself every week, paying as much as I could until the last evening, when I was able to take the accordian home with me. I am unable to express the excitement I felt to think that this marvellous instrument was mine. But alas, I found out that for me to read music was impossible; I had played the piano for so long by ear, that I could not follow the music. My teacher would hit the ceiling every time I put my own little fiddly bit in. So eventually I stopped having lessons and continued to play by ear. I got some books out of the library and learned the fundamentals about chords, but I was never brilliant. In all this time there seemed little interest from my parents.

Mr Palmer was a tyrant in the top class. When the boys were doing the sums he would walk round the desks. If a boy was not working, he would be made to stop in after school. If he saw a sum wrong, the boy received an unexpected clump round the ear. Mr Palmer was feared more than the headmaster. He was a tall man and used to wear a grey suit, always immaculately pressed, and his shoes shone like two mirrors on his feet. His steely grey hair was always in place; he reminded me of a military officer.

What went through his mind when he lined us up for inspection every morning, I can't imagine. There we were with our trodden-down shoes, the toes scraped and unpolished because our mothers didn't have the time, and being boys we didn't care anyway, our ragged coats and shirts, sometimes secondhand, and our socks full of holes. One boy, Trueman, from a very poor family, must have gone through a great deal of mental suffering. He had something wrong with his nose, and his nose would be continually running, and sometimes he didn't realise this and the boys would call him Snotty Trueman. Mr Palmer would bawl at him,

'Wipe your bloody nose, will you!'

He found it most difficult to make a friend.

I used to go to school at times when my breathing was quite bad. On these occasions I would have to climb about twelve flights of stairs to the top class: you couldn't get any higher than this. I would have to stop a number of times on the way to get my breath back. My head would start to ache and I would feel sick at the effort of trying to make it. When I eventually got to the top, I would wait until I had recovered before going into the classroom.

When my mother was first told by the doctor that I had asthma, she did not tell me. But on our arrival back at home, I heard her whisper to my father that I had asthma. Owing to the way she whispered to my father about it, I felt not only scared but ashamed of having such a thing. This is why I waited outside the classroom so that no one would know that I had asthma. I of course had to tell my teacher when I was off sick, but I have always felt inferior about it. Whether this is natural or not I don't know.

I was already late for school because of my slow pace. As well as feeling like I did, I was also afraid of what awaited me when I went into class. I was terrified of Mr Palmer and he was very strict on time.

On other ocasions when I felt ill, I would ask if I could stay in class during playtime, because I dreaded the great effort of climbing the stairs back up again. He agreed to the breaks, but he would never allow me to stay in class during lunch time, so I had this trip up the stairs at least twice a day.

I timidly entered the room. It was complete silence as usual. No boy would dare move when Mr Palmer had his eyes on them.

'Come here, Barnes! Where have you been?'

'I'm not well today, sir,' I said quietly, so that the boys could not hear.

'Speak up, boy, for heaven's sake! You are always late. Not a week goes by without you being late at least twice.'

I now had to ask him if I could stay in at playtime, a thing that would be a punishment for many boys.

'No, you cannot!' he said. Then he shouted,

'I think you're making this asthma thing of yours too much of an excuse!'

I felt belittled at him using the word asthma in front of all the class. At playtime I went down — the boys were all around me.

'You got asthma then, Barnsie. What is it?'

Another boy cut in,

'Oh, my old man's got that. He goes red in the face sometimes, then blue, you'd think he was dying sometimes, but he don't. He got it working on the gas board.'

When I came up the stairs I was struggling for breath. I had to stop many times. Kids were still asking,

'What's the matter with him, then?'

'Oh, he's got asthma.'

From the unfeeling attitude of Mr Palmer, I not only suffered physically; I had to be humiliated as well.

I had to accept the face that I would now have to go down to play whether I was sick or not. One playtime, I went into the toilet feeling sick through straining to get my breath. Some boys used to go in the toilets and make a terrible row, and the caretaker was always chucking them out and warning them that they would get a clump round the ear if they were caught again. On this occasion a crowd had congregated and I was in one of the stalls being sick. I heard the voice of the caretaker threatening the kids again, then it was complete silence. All the kids had gone. I then came out of the stalls. As I did so the caretaker was walking away from me. He must have heard the door shut, because he turned round and as he did so he looked furious.

'Come here, you little sod. Hide in there, would you?'

The next thing I felt was his big, hard hand slapping into my face. I didn't cry, I just stood there stunned and bewildered.

What makes a child become delinquent, they ask. What makes a child violent and hateful towards grown-ups, what makes him become a rebel and a crook? The crook is not politically aware, the rebel is, according to the psychiatrists. I should have been at least one of these things, but for some unknown reason I am not. I am aware of the injustices in life, between the classes, and I have been aware of the

16

rich and the poor with their different ways of life since a small child. What the poor child needs, yes and even some rich children, is love and understanding in this bewildering and violent place.

They are taught to be like Jesus, and suddenly an iron hand is smashed across their face. No wonder they are bewildered. No wonder they are violent. Their frustrations must have an outlet somewhere, so they smash windows, tear cinema seats, wreck cars and torture animals, because by doing these things they vent their anger, with no fear of retaliation.

After experiencing a man like Palmer, fate seemed to smile on me, for I had to go to an 'Open Air School', because I was frequently absent at the school I was at. As unhappy as I was at High Street School, I wasn't keen on leaving. I thought, what am I in for now? But I need not have worried.

The school was Gere House Open Air School in Stepney Green. I had to get a bus there from Stoke Newington on the Monday morning. I arrived alone, feeling rather tense. As I came into the playground, there were three sorts of bandstands. Not round like you see in the parks, but square, two standing together and one on its own. The two biggest ones were classrooms, one for the infants and one for the seniors. The other was the refectory. A big, fat nurse was coming towards me,

'Come on, boy, come with me. You are going to see the head-master before going into class.'

I must have been late, because no kids were in the playground. She seemed strict at first, but after getting used to her ways she was really quite likeable. I couldn't understand this, seeing the head-master. I hadn't come within fifty yards of the one at my previous school.

He was slim and quiet-spoken and there was no sign of sternness in him at all. I was completely taken aback to be spoken to in such an easy-going manner.

'Good morning, lad, glad to have you with us. Well, I hope you'll be happy here. Now, nurse will take you to your classroom, and don't forget, if there is anything worrying you, or if you have any problem at school, come and see me.'

I was transifxed in bewilderment.

'Come on, son.' The nurse was pulling at my arm. As we descended the stairs I was still in a stupor. 'Son', 'Lad', these affectionate titles I had never been given before, by teachers, parents or anyone else for that matter. If only people realised what warmth a child derive

17

from these affectionate terms, I am sure they would use them more often. In my previous school we were called by our second names only.

My new teacher, Mr Osbourne, was more like an elderly uncle. As soon as I set eyes on him I knew he was a man of great kindness and understanding. The council had done me a great favour by sending me to this school.

If a child could not understand a subject, Mr Osbourne would have the child at his desk and explain every detail over and over again, to each child individually if necessary. This man was a born teacher. I never saw him strike a child at any time: the kids loved and respected him. There was no bullying in the playground, although there were plenty of threats among the boys. I believe the reason for this non-violence among the boys was the fine example of Mr Osbourne.

When he saw that I was good at art he let me do as much as I wanted. When I wanted a rest from art I would join in the other lessons. Consequently, my painting improved considerably, but the other lessons I was never able to improve on at all.

Mr Osbourne was short and plump and in the winter he wore a thick coat. He wore a wide-rimmed trilby hat which came well down on his forehead. If it were not for his glasses and rather large ears, the hat would have come down right over his face. And he had a large nose. As you can see, he was no Errol Flynn, but to us he was the greatest. A complete opposite of the military Mr Palmer.

One lad in school was a cripple. If he fell over he was unable to get up again. When we played football he was always put in goal, although he used to insist that he should play on the field. Behind his back, when the boys used to pick their teams, they would say,

'No, I don't bleeding want him. 'e can't even run, and if he falls we've got to leave the ball and keep picking him up.'

I was standing by the classroom door one dinner-time. It was quiet and I heard sobbing. It was the crippled boy and I heard Mr Osbourne saying,

'What do you mean, they don't want you on the field because you're a cripple? Who's the best in the class at music, or arithmetic, or history? Do you want to be good at everything, then?'

'No, sir.'

'Well you can't. In any case, I think, in fact I'm sure, they want you in goal because that is what you're good at. And to prove it, I'm going to ask the boys after dinner.'

18

On over-hearing this, I rounded up the boys and told them that Mr Osbourne was going to ask them why the boy was not wanted on the field. I then told them to say that it was because he was too good in goal. At the same time I informed them that any boy saying different to this would have his guts smashed in after school. Whether I could have achieved such a thing I never found out because they all stuck to that story. The crippled boy remained in goal happy ever after.

I suppose I defended this boy as I did because I could relate to him, and I suppose many others in the school must have felt the same way. The boys who didn't want them on their side couldn't very well tell him to his face. I mean they couldn't very well say,

'Look here, we don't want a cripple in our team.'

This is what many disabled people have to go through in their search for employment. There are many people who go to work who are disabled, but nobody pays any attention to them Why? Because their disability cannot be seen.

I was sent to school in Woodford, a boarding school. I was about twelve at the time. This was the first time that I had been away from both my parents and it was a great shock to me. It was a convent run by nuns.

My parents walked me up the long path towards the two great oak doors. My mother pulled the lever to ring the bell and we waited a few moments. The left hand door slowly opened to reveal an elderly nun. Her apparel frightened the wits out of me − I had never seen a nun before. A few words were exchanged and I was left alone, terrified of what was in store for me. The nun seemed to grasp my hand ever so tightly; she was taking me to get some sandals, a pull-over and some shorts.

I was then introduced to Mr Roberts. He was the bloke who kept the boys in order and organised games. He was an ex-army man, short of stature, with a bald head, thick neck and ruddy face. Not what you would call angelic. We were standing in the field.

'Wait there a minute, lad,' he said.

He disappeared into the washrooms and then I heard a wacking noise and howls. I learned later from the victim that he got this punishment for not washing behind his ears after being warned a number of times. He got it on the bare buttocks with a hair brush.

My fear of the nuns was unnecessary. These women are really beautiful in their face and in their ways. Not one word of threat or scorn did I receive from them in the whole three months I was there.

I was unlucky enough to receive a wasp sting one day, while playing cricket. I went directly to the clinic, crying with pain. The medic was a nun. She dressed the sting with iodine, and to my surprise and joy, she took me in her arms and comforted me. I thought, getting a sting isn't so bad after all.

There was a nun and another woman who ran the kitchen. The nun would clear up and set the tables and the other woman would cook and wash up. They seemed to take to me and asked me if I would like to help each day and told me I would get an extra sweet ration in return. I jumped at the offer. The two of them would argue with each other; one wanted me to help her in the kitchen and the other wanted me in the refectory. This made me feel great; never before had anyone argued over me like this. But this may have been put on for my benefit: perhaps they could see how lost I felt, even after about six weeks at the school.

I hated salad. We were all standing by the tables in the refectory, and had just said grace. Mr Roberts was saying,

'There's been too much talking at table lately. Any boy talking will feel the weight of my hand.'

I heard none of this because my mind was on the salad in front of me. I was afraid that I would be forced to eat it, for I knew that if I was I would bring it all up. I turned to a boy asking him,

'Can you eat my salad?'

Suddenly I saw complete blackness and then a lightning flash. After a few moments I recovered and realised that Roberts had smashed one of his iron hands into my face. No tears were shed, just a feeling of numbness, confusion and insecurity. Until that is, the nun in charge of the refectory came over to me after the meal, when everybody had gone, and held me in her arms saying,

'Come here, my baby, you didn't deserve it my love, never, never mind.'

I was happy once again, and all fear had gone.

Time came round for me to go home. I had not had one attack of asthma all the three months I was there. As soon as I came home, to bad housing, family tension, holes in shoes, and all the rest, I was back to where I started.

Just after the war, I must have been about eleven at the time, a gang of us kids used to play in Darville Road on one of the bomb sites. There was one certain kid who was not allowed to play on these places and whose parents didn't really want him playing with us. We used to say that he was posh because his parents owned their house, had a car and ran their own business. The boy would always be clean and well-dressed, and perhaps this was one of the reasons we didn't like him too much and why we didn't accept him into our group at first. He used to talk, as we would say, posh, and this didn't exactly help us to have any feelings of friendship towards him. He was unfortunate to be given the name Poshit by the boys; what this name was supposed to convey I don't know.

He would have to be in at seven in the evening and no later. Although we weren't too keen on him coming into the group at first, we eventually got round to liking him.

'He's not a bad kid.' said one of the boys, 'even though he can't stay out like us till eleven at night, and he can't help it if he has to walk about tidy and all that, and speak posh. We should think ourselves lucky we ain't got parents like that!'

'Hear! Hear!' we all shouted.

Poshit we accepted, but his parents we could not stand, the feeling was mutual.

I can remember after I left school my mother would be up at six in the morning, to get to work at the Imperial Tobacco Company by eight o'clock. Before that she had to get breakfast and tidy up. She would arrive home about seven in the evening, sometimes six-thirty if she didn't have to wait too long for a bus. She would do this five days a week, summer and winter, sweating in the factory amongst the dust and the smell, nine hours a day. Saturdays and Sundays were spent shopping, cooking and clearing up. She would be lucky if she got a rest on Sunday afternoon. During the week she would probably have about one and a half or two hours' rest before going to bed.

She would work like this, not for extra money for luxuries, but to supplement my father's poor wage. I saw her go from a strapping fourteen stone to eight stone during the years of my childhood. My father would start work at two in the afternoon and finish at ten at night: the only real time we could be together would be of a Sunday. I believe this was one of the factors in the breaking up of their marriage.

I can remember when my mother would come home after having some teeth out and have to stand cooking dinner for us. This went on for about a month until all her teeth were extracted. How she was able to endure this after a day's work and then cook the dinner, do the housework and go back to the factory the next morning, I shall never know.

I loved my parents completely. But somehow I could not help feeling a sense of distance between us. I used to wonder why they never showed any affection towards each other; perhaps they did, but I never saw it. I often wished I could see them embrace. Although I am sure they loved me and tried to do all they could to make me happy, there always seemed to be a barrier between us. They seemed to me more like friends. I realise now that things weren't easy for them at that time, and we also have to take into account their own home life as children, which I'm sure could not have been rosy in the thirties, living in the East End in a street like Poyser Street.

My mother had been brought up in a good home, her father earning a little more than the average at that time. They were able to have nice furniture and this has always made my mother want a nice place. My father was brought up in somewhat poorer conditions, and nice furniture and so on did not seem to worry him. He did not seem to like laying out for new furniture or clothes; everything he bought would have to be secondhand, because this is how he had to live when he was a child.

Like many poor families in those days, we never had a summer holiday. My summer Sundays would be spent playing down Darville Road, my father asleep in the armchair after dinner, my mother getting what rest she could before starting her routine — making tea, washing up and clearing up, my father never offering to help at all. Life for my mother was very hard. This is probably why she didn't have much time for me and when she did have time it had to be spent in resting ready for the next lot of work. My parents hardly went out together, either because they did not have the money or the energy, or because they had had a row.

I can remember just before the war, my Dad used to take bets in Poyser Street. His little brother, Johnny, always used to play up there. He must have been about nine years old at the time. He was always in the habit of wearing his trousers three or four times too big for him. For a belt he would always use one of his mother's old stockings. My dad used to carry a penknife on him and at the first opportunity he would get behind Johnny and with a quick flick of the knife the stocking was severed. The trousers, being rather large, would immediately fall. My dad would cry, 'Gotcha!' Johnny would scream some abuse, hoist up his trousers and sprint home for another stocking. Whenever my dad was about, Johnny would keep a wary eye on him all the time. But he could stand this mental stress no longer, and one day he turned up with a pair of braces.

This solved his problem completely.

I will never forget the day when he got nicked for taking bets. If he saw a copper coming, in or out of uniform, he would run into Jim Barber's house. Jim was an elderly, miserable man, but he saved dad from many a nicking. But this time dad was not quick enough. The copper was behind him, as though he had come up out of the ground. I didn't take much notice at first, but when I saw how the copper took my dad by the back of the neck to the station, I hated his guts. But what could I have done.

About the same time my Aunt Polly moved next door to us at 38 Brooke Road. Of course we were always in and out of their house and they were in and out of ours. But we both lived on the top floor and it got a bit tedious to keep going up and down, just to ask each other when we were going out or something like that. So what did my father do? He made a hole, about an inch in diameter, right through the wall. This made communications a lot easier, but this new found system had its drawbacks.

If you happened to be sitting near the hole, or just happen to pass it, you would never know when a jet of water, or perhaps a poker, was coming through at you.

My two cousins, Audrey and Iris, would talk to me through this hole. They would tap on the wall to me and shout, 'Through the hole!' I would immediately answer the signal and go to the hole to receive their message. One afternoon they called me in this fashion. I of course went to the hole like always.

'Look through!' they shouted.

I did, pressing my eye firmly to it, only to have it spat in.

I wiped my eye and thought, right, now for revenge. I waited until the incident was forgotten. A week or so went by and my Uncle George was just coming home from the navy. He always used to keep his uniform spotless and well pressed. I waited till Sunday afternoon to reap my revenge on my two cousins. I knew that then they would all be lounging in the armchairs after dinner. I took a teaspoon of flour, held the spoon to the hole, and blew heartily. The screams and cries told me that my weapon had had the desired effect. Their kitchen was one floury haze. I could just see through the hole what was going on. My aunt Polly shouted,

'I bet it's that little sod next door!'

I wonder how she knew that. The only problem was that my poor uncle was sitting right in line of fire and his uniform was now a speckled white.

My Uncle George who lived next door to us at Brooke Road, was a totter for some time, and had his own horse and cart. In the summer, usually on a Sunday, he would take all the family for a ride and a day out to Epping Forest. The cart was only very small, and so popular were these outings with the family, that everyone would turn up for this treat. The cart would be crammed full to capacity with Barnes's and their wives and children. You'd hardly be able to move, and the poor horse really had a job on. But Uncle George would let her take her own time and once we were at Epping, Mary would have a good day's rest until the evening.

Going, I would be sitting up the front with my accordian, and there'd be singing and jokes all the way. When they got there it would be straight in the pub and when that closed out would come the sandwiches and pickles. After a rest, to let it all go down, someone would suggest a game of cricket or something else.

I can remember at one time a fairground, I don't think it was Epping, my uncle had had a few, and he decided to have a pony ride. The animal was more like a stallion than a pony. After managing to persuade the owner that he was sober enough to handle the horse, Uncle George mounted, though rather ungracefully. The horse went steadily away, as the family looked on with apprehension, then it broke into a trot, and finally a gallop. Uncle was really enjoying himself, showing off his horse-riding skills, then it happened. Suddenly, without warning, uncle was now under the belly of the horse, and the horse still pelting away. We were all in fits of laughter.

'Blimey,' someone said, 'he rides like a bleeding Cossack, don't he?' Pretending that he didn't realise that this stunt of Uncle George's was unintentional. And round and round he went, until the horse had had enough and galloped back to the starting point and came to a sudden halt. Uncle landed on his back. I think this incident had a very sobering effect on him, for there wasn't another word out of him for a couple of hours after.

Mary, his horse, used to know every pub that Uncle George used to stop at. On one occasion, I think it was around Christmas, he got well soaked. He staggered on to the cart and Mary pulled away. Uncle finished up in the back of the cart and Mary brought him all the way home. God knows how long he had been laying in the cart outside the house before my aunt, who was getting a bit worried about him, looked out of the window.

'Well, look at that drunken sod out there. Let's go and get him.'

He was a very big man and what a time they had getting him off the cart and into the house.

He would leave a lot of his stock from totting in the yard downstairs, although the man downstairs wasn't too keen on this practice. One day uncle thought he would give up the totting trade and go in for fruit and vegetables. So along came his cart filled with his new merchandise which he then unloaded into the yard as well. The Hyde Park Horse Show was not far ahead now and uncle would never miss this occasion. This time he had something different in mind. He decided he would make a small cart, get a nanny goat, and let me ride in front of him at the show. The cart was soon put together and painted.

The next thing was the nanny goat. Down 'the lane' he went on the Sunday morning, and in no time at all he was back with a nanny goat. And need I say where he kept it? Of course, in the yard. But all our hopes were to be dashed to the ground. The man downstairs had just come home from the pub, ready for his Sunday dinner. He sat at a table facing the window, which was open for it was rather a hot day. Suddenly the eyes of the goat were looking straight into his, as his fork went to his mouth.

'Mabel, Mabel!' he screamed. 'Am I bleeding well seeing things, or am I that drunk I'm beginning to see white goats?'

His wife knew nothing about the animal.

'What are you talking about? Goats, goats, what goats?'

'A bleeding goat looked in at me, didn't you see it?'

'Oh, don't be daft,' she said. 'Who'd bring a goat in the house?' She forgot about my uncle when she said this.

There was no knowing what he would bring home next. When my aunt used to see him draw up loaded with gear, she'd say,

'Oh, gor blimey, what's coming into the house now?'

Anyway, after the downstairs tenants had got over the initial shock and gone into the yard to confirm what the husband had said, up they came to us upstairs. Bang! Bang! on the door. My uncle was shaving at the time. He opened the door with his left hand and was lathering up with his right.

'Now, look here, George. You've made an old iron yard out of it. You've made a Spitalfields Market out of it, but you're not making a bleeding cattle market out of it as well. That bloody thing's got to go.'

Now George stopped lathering.

'But there's plenty of room out there for half a dozen goats, mate.'

'Oh, yeah, you just try it then. I'm not having that flea-bag poking its head in at me every time I have a meal. If it's not out of here tonight, I'm getting in touch with the landlord.'

He then smartly turned about and walked down.

Uncle George, holding the lather brush to his face, was left in deep thought, puzzled at why this man should have become so antagonistic towards him. If you think that this is unbelievable then listen to what happened next.

George would not get rid of the goat then because it was Sunday.

'All right,' he said, 'we'll bring it up here.'

'Up here!' my aunt screamed.

'Well it's only for tonight ain't it?'

We had a terrible time getting that nanny up the steep wooden staircase, but after much bleating from this poor animal, and volumes of swearing from my uncle, calling the man downstairs all manner of names, suggesting the doubtful character of himself and his mother, the goat was safely got upstairs. And this put paid to my uncle's plan. He just could not imagine what harm there was in having the goat in the back yard.

My uncle was a real character. For a few weeks he would be loaded with money and do the lot. But he always looked after the kids first, and the rest he enjoyed himself. If he had no money, he wouldn't be without it long. His ingenuity for acquiring money had no end, whether it was by fair means or foul. He was never what you would call broke.

# 3

I wanted to be a sign-writer. If I had had the right guidance, I would have wanted to be an artist, but to me sign-writing was an art. I got a reference from school which no employer even looked at and I found it very difficult to get a job as an apprentice, or even a learner.

'Well,' said Mum. 'You'd better go into the french polishing with Uncle Alf, then.'

My mother had always been a bit of a mystery to me. Here I was, an asthmatic child, being told by my mother to take up french polishing, among the fumes of polish, sawdust, and in very bad working conditions. All I could put this down to was that she didn't understand what sort of trade she was telling me to go into.

At last I managed to get a job from the labour, as a learner sign-writer in Stamford Hill. I rang the bell and waited. I then heard footsteps running down the stairs as though being chased. When the door came open I was then faced with the enormous body of Mr Davis. I never thought it possible for a man of his build to run downstairs like this.

'I'm enquiring about the job.'

'Oh yes, how old are you?'

'Fourteen, sir.'

'Don't call me sir, boy, for gawd's sake. No sir, er, Mr Davis 'll do.'

'I have a reference here from my school. They think I would be suited to sign-writing.'

'Oh, never mind that, can you make tea?'

'Yes, sir – Mr Davis.'

'Are you strong?'

'Oh, yes s . . .'

'Do you think you could lift scaffold boards and push a barrow?'

'Oh yes, I could.'

I was hoping that my tone of voice would make me appear stronger than I looked.

'All right, kid, start Monday.'

Oh boy.

'Thank you sir Davis, er Mr Davis, thank you.'

I was full of joy that afternoon. Never again was I to experience the delight and sense of achievement that I got from getting my first job. I had visions of becoming a first class tradesman, with my own little box of paints and first class brushes and a palette. As soon as my parents came home I told them. Their reply was 'Oh good'. No questions, nothing. My mother wasn't on to me to start work to get some money from me, but it did hurt me deeply when little interest was shown at what I thought was a wonderful achievement. Maybe they were so depressed with their life of work and struggle and an unhappy marriage, that they could find no enthusiasm for anything. Or they may have been just plain indifferent. I don't know.

I reported for work on Monday morning at 8 a.m. I made my way down the sloping alleyway, which was about five hundred yards long. I got to the bottom and there was the shed on the left. All around were scaffold boards, ladders and old shop facias. The two big doors to the shed were open. I looked inside to see two men, one about fifty and the other about twenty-five. The older man spotted me.

'Are you the new boy, then?'

'Yes, sir.'

'I'm Alf and him there is Ron. What's yours?'

'Er, my name's Ron as well.'

'Ah, be jasus, we can't have that now, can we? There's enough fucking confusion around here already. We'll call you Ronald. You ever used a brush, have you?' said Alf.

'Well, I have done a lot of drawing and painting and that.'

'Well forget all that, 'cause you won't be doing any drawing here. Do yer know the primary colours?' he asked.

'I do,' I replied.

'Have you ever mixed oil colours?'

'No, sir.'

'Alf, not sir!' he bawled. 'Well first of all you'd better make a cup of tea.'

This Irish foreman, Alf, was short but heavily built, with a mass of thick, curly black hair, a broad face, wide-set clear blue eyes, broad nose and a healthy red face. Although he only stood about five foot four, he was a fit and powerful man.

He showed me how to mix paints, and this was my job for a

long time, before ever touching a sign-writing brush. After being there about five months I had still not been given the opportunity to use a writer. I thought, perhaps Alf doesn't think I could do it? At home I did a poster, and was inspired to write, 'God is Love'. It turned out beautiful. I thought that if I showed it to Alf he might have a better opinion of me. I couldn't have been more wrong.

'Oh, gawd, bloody blimey. Oh holy mother of God! What are you trying to do: convert me or something? Oh fucking hell, oh it's fucking good boy, fucking good to be sure!'

About a fortnight after this incident, I had a chance to try my hand on some ladders which had the firm's name on them and had to be gone over to liven them up a bit.

'Now then, Ron. I've got to go out on a job, find something for Ronald to do.'

Alf picked up his kit, made his way down the alley and disappeared.

'I know what you can do, Ronald,' said Ron. 'You can paint over the firm's name on them ladders.'

'What me?' I said.

'Yes. But you'll have to keep your eye open for him coming back. At least it's something for you to practise on, and anyway, there's nothing else for you to do.'

I mixed up my paints, got out the ladders, got a box to sit on, and away I went. After a while I could feel I was being watched. I slowly turned round and a few yards behind me was Ron.

'Good kid good. Look, Ronald, take no notice of him.'

'Oh Alf you mean.'

'Who else?' said Ron.

He came nearer so that he was right behind me.

'He's a funny bloke.' he said. 'Mind you he treated me rough when I first started, but what he did to you the other week was daibolical. But never mind kid you keep at it and you'll soon pick it up. It's easy enough writing when you've got the knack, but wait till you have to get up there on those bleeding scaffold boards with a force nine gale blowing up your arse, or when the sun plays on your back till you want to spew your ring up. And the bright colours don't help your eyes much; that's why old Alf's got a squint ain't it? Keep at it son.'

I had been writing for about an hour. Ron had just gone to put an order in for some colours at the office above our shed. Suddenly

I felt someone behind me. It can't be Ron, I thought, he's in the office. Oh no, it can't be comrade Alf. I shouldn't have got so carried away with the job in hand. I slowly turned my head. As I did so, Alf's chin was almost resting on my left shoulder.

'Don't they look attractive enough for you' he said. 'And what makes you think your bleeding wobbly hand is going to improve them? What a liberty you've got. Wipe it off. Ron,' he bawled, 'come here!'

I was sweating hot and cold, and I felt I had committed a most terrible crime.

'Don't you dare let him do that fucking lark anymore, I'm telling you. In fact next time I've got a job outside **you** will come with me.'

What was going through his mind I was soon to find out during that same week.

'Righto! Ronald get that barrow.!

To me this barrow was a monster on iron treaded wheels of about three feet diameter.

'Now then get those four boards and four tressels and put them on the cart.'

The boards were about two inches thick, and about eight foot long. The tressels were about ten foot long. Ron could see how exhausted I was after the first three boards and made towards me.

'Leave him!' screamed Alf. 'He wants to be a sign writer so he's got to know how to handle ladders and push a barrow.'

Ron gave Alf a look of hatred, but said nothing, probably because if he did his life would be made a misery as well, or perhaps the sack, the most dreaded weapon of all. I finally lifted the last tressel onto the barrow.

'Now then' shouted Alf, 'put me coat on, that bucket and rags, and me kit. O.K. Ron we will see you tonight. I painted the shop front yesterday and I'm going to finish it today, I've got to write and varnish it. Right now then' he said, 'push like fuck!'

I look up the slope of the alleyway and thought god I'll never make that, the weight on the barrow must have been about seven hundredweight. Alf pushed it like wheeling a baby in a pram. As we got half way up the slope Alf eased off so that I had most of the weight.

'Come on' he shouted, 'don't leave it all to me'.

I couldn't even see over the barrow, if I was going straight or not, I was on the kerb side; the barrow must have moved out to the right when a bus just missed the front of the barrow as it passed. Alf

30

jumped up like he was going into a complicated ballet step.

'Keep the fucking thing straight' he bawled. A woman must have heard this language as she passed, judging by the look of surprise on her face.

We eventually got the job in Stoke Newington High Street. By this time I was sweating profusely, off came our coats and we began to put up our tressels. Alf got out his brushes and colours, made his way up the steps and settled down to write, leaving me at the bottom. I began to cool down and I began to feel cold.

'Alf! I'm breaking me neck' I called.

'Go in the shop, sod you, and ask if you can use theirs'.

I was to make this journey many times in the course of the day. Whether Alf's guardian angel spoke to him or not I don't know, but he shouted to me to come up to him. I had never been on a scaffold before, it must have been about twenty foot up, not very high, but for a novice it seemed about twice that height. I held on for dear life. As I got to the top of the tressels, and had to swing my leg over and onto the boards.

'Come on' cried Alf, 'don't shit your fucking self, just don't look down'.

I didn't want him to think I was scared so I stood as upright as I could, and made towards him. Then it happened: I had trodden on a part where two boards were over-lapping. I did a sort of tap dance where the performer leans the body forward and kicks back his legs alternately. There was Alf doubled over, holding his stomach, red in the face with glee, the happiest I had ever seen him, he was overcome with joy. His joy was quickly broken when on recovering himself he found his front covered in the red paint which was meant for the job. Where he had been leaning over, the small pots clipped to his pallet had tilted, the paint running down the front of his overalls.

'You clumsy git' he said, 'go down and get a cloth off the barrow. No, don't bother I'll go'.

After wiping himself down, he then gave me a brush and I was allowed to paint the inside of the letters, while Alf did the more skilled job of doing the outlines of the letters. After letting me do this my spirits began to rise, with visions of myself carrying my little box, with its paint and oils and brushes inside. I began to make my own sign-writing box, in my spare time in the yard, when I didn't have to mix paints or make boards for the shop fronts. But for some unknown reason Alf would harrass me at every occasion and try to dishearten me. At times I would go home through the back streets so as to hide my tears from passers-by. I was so unhappy with this man after me all the time, yet I was afriad to pack up in case I couldn't get another job in the sign-writing trade; heaven knows it was difficult enough getting this job let alone a second choice. I was unable to tell my parents my troubles, as they always seemed to be so distant, why I don't know, but there it was. So, when in bed I would pray, I had always prayed. God? I didn't even feel that I knew him or his son, there was no one else, so I prayed. Well, they told me in school to pray if I wanted something, so that's what I did. I got no answer. Alf kept after me, and I had to pack up, I could stand no more. Mr Davis could do nothing about it.

So much for job number one.

'I don't know why you don't go in for french polishing with your Uncle Alf,' my mother would say. After being out for about three months, I tried a little sign-writing shop in Stoke Newington Church Street. The owner didn't want to know if I could make tea, in fact he didn't want to know anything. 'Bring your cards on Monday' and that was it.

He was a big man with a big beard and of more gentle breeding than Alf. One mistake lost me this golden opportunity to learn the trade. Jackson had a small board to write in De Beauvoir Road. He gave me a large empty paint can, and a small one full of paint which was to paint the background with before writing. He also gave me some newspaper and said,

'Put the newspaper in the large can and then put the small tin of paint inside the big one.'

Due to my misunderstanding, I thought he wanted the small tin poured on to the newspaper that had been put in the large can, and this is what I did, thinking it was some kind of trade trick that I hadn't seen yet. When I had finished painting the board it looked shocking. Result: the sack.

# 4

I hunted around for another job, but this time it was impossible. I couldn't find a sign-writing job anywhere. I broke the news to my mother.

'Well I told you to go in the french polishing, didn't I?' she said.

Well I had no interest in french polishing, but it would be something until I could get into the sign-writing, and the money was good, even for a learner, at three bob an hour.

I arrived on the Monday morning at Kings Cabinet Co. in Kingsland Road. I walked through the saw mill amid the noise and dust, shavings clinging to the bottom of my trousers and dust getting in my shoes; I wondered how on earth these men with their dusty caps and faces and leather aprons, stuck this sort of work. On talking, or should I say, shouting to one of them on my way through, I asked this question.

'Oh,' he bawled, 'it's all right. We gets plenty of milk to wash it down with.'

I proceeded up a flight of dangerously steep stairs. As I came to the top, the polishing shop was ahead of me, and to my right was the cabinetmakers'. An old Jewish maker came towards me, short and tubby, his shabby clothes laden with dust, as well as his walrus moustache. He had one eye peering through the dust of his glasses. He looked like an antique model of an old man that had been left laying somewhere and had gathered dust.

'For vot you vant?' he asked.

'I want the polishers'.'

'Ah, de polishers is op dere. Ask for Joe, he is de piece-master.'

A piece-master is one who gets paid for each piece he turns out. He buys his own materials and takes on his own staff; he must get as much out of them as he can, for as little as possible.

I walked forward about ten yards and then entered the polishing shop. The choking stench of polish stain and tea hit me. I became short of breath and used my inhaler. The polishing shop was about

twenty feet long and about fifteen feet wide. The shop was fairly
well lit — all polishing shops have to be for the matching up of
colours. It was cold and damp and dusty; polish lay thick on the
grey, decrepit walls, where the workers had rubbed excess polish out
of their polishing rubbers. Unfinished cabinets lay strewn all over
the place, as though someone was shifting their furniture around.

Sam was the first one I spoke to. He was what they call 'fadding
up'. He was about sixteen, one of the biggest boys I've ever seen. He
was singing at the top of his voice, his big thick hands gripping the
panel he was polishing, his hands caked with dry polish. As soon as
he spotted me, he stopped singing and laughed:

'What, are you the new kid, then?'

I looked up at this giant, 'Er, yes.'

'John!' he yelled. 'The new kid's here.'

A head wearing a trilby hat peered round the side of a cabinet
at the end of the shop. A hand then appeared, covered in black satin.
It beckoned me forward and then disappeared. I made towards the
cabinet and went to the front. I began to picture Sam, and wondered
why a boy should grow so big, strong and healthy who had lived the
same sort of life as I had, in the East End, father out of work and the
rest of it. His face was ruddy. But now I was faced with an older
face of about forty, which was long and drawn, sagging at the cheeks
and under the eyes, white shiny skin, waxy. This face was full of
worry and fatigue. I suppose this was through the worry of being a
piece-master, having to find the wages for staff week after week, as
well as having to turn out a certain number of jobs each week.

John was kneeling, a brush in his right hand extended forward on
to the carcase he was colouring. He slowly rose, holding his back
with his free hand. He was about five foot three in his trilby hat,
which never left his head. Behind me was Bill, about the same age
as John, but even smaller than his master, and the same sallow complexion. Bill was an expert, in the game; he was not only a first class
colourer, but like lightning as well. John was the boss, but it took
him all his time to keep up with this dynamic little chap.

John looked at me as though I had rudely interrupted him.

'What's your name, son?'

'Ron', I said.

'Right, then, I'm John, he's Bill, and Sam's up there. Go and
help him do some staining.'

I reported to Sam.

'Well, ain't yer got an overall, then?'

'Well, no.'

'Gor blimey, take that old one there.'

It wasn't really an overall, but a big white apron with two pockets in the front. It was about twenty times too big for me and not even white. It was more like a dark oak colour, the polish laying thickly upon it so that the oil in the material soaked through to my trousers. I discovered when I got home that it had gone through to my skin.

'Right,' said Sam. 'Get that pot of stain and do all the carcases as the makers bring them up.'

I looked a real craftsman in my apron, which completely covered my shoes. I kept this up for about two hours, the stain making me feel bilious with headache.

'Oh, you'll get used to that,' said Sam.

I daren't say anything about my asthma.

A bell rang out. Sam made one dash, as though making a desperate escape from a bank robbery.

'Come on, mate, ten o'clock, grub.'

Bill was sitting on a box which was covered with innumerable layers of polish. His black, stained hands were grasping a thick slice of bread and dripping, wrapped in a piece of paper for the sake of hygiene. John had the same and so did Sam who was sitting on the stain pot with a board over it. The only difference was that his large slice of bread looked but a crumb in those large, thick stained fingers of his. His great mouth envelloped slice after slice; he devoured six in all.

'Blimey, bleeding smashing,' he said, as he picked up his stained, cracked mug of tea.

This fellow was a real giant at the side of his two fellow diners, who could only nibble feebly at these great slices. Sam spoke,

'Come on, Ron, get stuck in.'

I felt sick and ill.

'But I haven't washed my hands.'

'Wash your 'ands. Gor blimey, we ain't got time to wash our 'ands mate, we only get ten minutes. Come on, draw up a pot or something to sit on and get stuck in.'

'No thanks, I don't feel hungry anyway.'

After two months of staining I was then promoted, if you can call it that, to sandpapering the insides of the cabinets and then putting a layer of polish on with a piece of wadding called a 'fad'. When doing this job, my head was inside the cabinet; the dust coming off the inside of the cabinet got on to my hair, into my eyes, up my nose and down my throat. When putting the polish on, the fumes would be stronger because your head was right inside there with the fad. I thought, well at least I've been allowed to use polish.

The months rolled by and I was still not to the fadding up stage. This is actually working on the exterior of the cabinet, bringing up a shine and bringing out the colour, so that the colourer, that is John and Bill, could match up the grain in the wood — a very skilful job indeed.

'Not yet,' came the reply. 'We've got to get this lot out fast.'

After asking this question and getting the same reply time and time again I gave up. By now my interest in sign-writing had faded and I was now keen to learn the french-polishing trade. The only way I could get my hand in was when John and Bill went to dinner, leaving Sam and myself alone. Sam would be sitting on the window ledge whistling the girls, and I would be getting to work, trying to learn the art of polishing. By doing this I eventually learnt to bring an expert shine to these cabinets, but I daren't let John know about this.

One day as they came up the stairs from dinner, John was saying to Bill,

'Yeah, if yer teaches 'em too much, they piss off and goes somewhere else and gets more money, and then you've got to get another kid and show him the ropes all over again. No, take yer time wiv 'em.'

He must have thought that Sam and me had gone out to dinner and weren't back yet, but it seemed that he did not know that I'd heard him. I quickly stopped what I was doing and picked up a stain rag. I had not quite finished polishing the cabinet I was working on but thought that when John had settled down at the other end of the shop, I could finish it, because once he started colouring he never stopped until tea.

I was sure it was safe now, so I continued on the cabinet, but I didn't reckon with Sam.

'Put that bleeding fad down, will yer, and stain those sodding cabinets. We've got to get them out by tea-time.'

I ignored Sam. Suddenly I was grabbed by my shirt at the shoulder and felt myself swiftly travelling in the direction of the unstained cabinets. I hit one with a bump, and my head was spinning when I tried to get up. Three or four cabinets had been badly damaged, and the noise and clatter had disturbed John, who came running, faster than I thought he was capable of. He couldn't have been more than thirty-eight, but he looked much older. Half bent from con-

tinually stooping to his work, white-faced, his eyes always heavy,
and always suffering with his stomach, which he blamed on the
fumes from the polish.

'What the bleedin' hell is going on, here?'

He could see I was dazed. He looked hatefully at Sam.

'Are you starting your tricks again? The other kid left over you,
you rotter.'

Sam tried to explain,

'Well he . . . '

'Never mind,' said John. 'I took you on from the probation
officer, to give you a chance to learn a trade and earn good money.
I've had enough of your cockiness and violence, so you can get out
now!'

'O.K.' said Sam. 'You're the boss.' And took off his apron.

'Yes, I am,' came the reply . .

Whether John put him off for roughing me up, I don't know, but
he was classed as skilled and now I was being asked to do his job.

'Come on,' said John. 'Pick up his fad and polish those cabinets
he was doing.'

'But I've never done it before,' I replied.

'You've seen him do it, ain't yer, well now you have a go.'

I was then doing Sam's job for less money. As time went on I
was polishing the cabinets as well as staining: in fact doing two
people's jobs. I approached John on this, who replied,

'Look, I've put out an ad for a young boy. Give us a few days
and we'll be all right again.'

No mention at all about more money. When I did ask for more
money it was always,

'Well, you're not skilled enough yet, boy. Give yourself a chance.'

I could see that when the new boy came and learnt the ropes, I
would get my rise and then the sack. So what did I do? You've
guessed, I'm sure. I jacked it in.

John was flabbergasted.

'You've got the chance to learn a good trade, with good money,
and am I hard on you, boy? You have a tea-break morning and
afternoon and you've got a bucket of soda water to wash your
'ands in before you go home. What do you kids want?'

Before this, I had tried to conceal my asthma on the days that I
went in feeling ill. I went in feeling like this in case I got put off.
And if I had been off too frequently, John would probably have
said,

'You'd better pack up, boy, the fumes are no good for you.'

But only if he had had another boy to replace me with. So far I had been lucky.

# 5

I stayed in the polishing game until I was seventeen; until I
realised how bad the trade was for my health. By this time I was one
of the spivs, as the lads were called in those days. I was now earning
the grand sum of five shillings an hour, which was really good money
at that time. I was able to give my mother more than my father was
able to.

I could afford to go down the lane in Cheshire Street and buy
myself a rig-out on one of the second-hand clothing stalls. You could
get some really classy stuff down there: a jacket, three bob or so, and
a pair of trousers, half a crown. Sometimes I would make an error in
the size, and if the jacket was too big, the stall-holder wasn't going
to notice it too easily and, having no mirror, a mistake was quite
easily made.

The jacket I had bought seemed rather large in the shoulders
when I got home with it. Luckily, the style then was draped jackets
with large shoulders. Without hesitation, I sorted out two of my
mother's stockings, stuffed them with rags and sewed them into the
jacket at the shoulders. This pulled the sleeves up, which were rather
long anyway, and caused me to look massive in the shoulders; I didn't
realise how massive.

I got myself ready on the Saturday night to meet the boys at our
regular meeting place: the Dalston fairground. This fair used to be
there all through the winter months. In summer it would be at
Clissold Park where all the boys would meet.

I made towards the group of boys who were standing near the
entrance. As I approached I seemed to catch their eye.

'Blimey, look at them shoulders!' cried Toenail, real name Tony.
'He looks like one of those timber humpers on the barges at the
canal.'

'When he gives you the cold shoulder,' giggled one, 'you know
you've bleeding got it.'

'Come here,' said Kununker. This boy leaned to one side all the time; he had an accident while playing in the street, a card had knocked him down, and this had left him paralysed on one side. Hence the name Kununker. He grabbed at my shoulder with his good arm and shook it ferociously. I felt the cotton break.

'Surely that's not all you, is it?' he said.

'Get off out of it!' I shouted.

The rest of the boys were in fits by now and they all joined in with Kununker, shaking my shoulders and pulling me about generally.

'On the cake-walk with him, boys!' came the cry from Chopper Mosely.

The cotton in my padding had now completely given way under this heavy handling. The cake-walk finished the job. The padding was gradually jerked and jolted down my sleeves and it was now dropping from the tail of my coat.

'Look!' they shouted. 'He's falling to pieces, he's all rags and stockings!'

'Blimey, you've got a right tailor, ain't you?'

As I was jolted to the end of the cake-walk, one of the boys handed me a brassiere which must have been part of my padding.

'I think you dropped this, Barnsie!' he screamed breathless with paroxysms of laughter.

I now stood, shoulders sagging, my hands completely hidden under my sleeves and my hair ruffled. I didn't know whether to shout abuse, run or threaten. The laughing died down. They were completely silent as though shocked at what they had done. Nobody moved. Chopper came over to me,

'Come on, Ron, you'd better go home and tidy up.'

He took hold of my arm. I shook him off roughly, turned my back and slowly walked away. I was glad I turned at that time for now the tears had spilled over my eyes.

The best part of the lives of these teenage boys was spent in strolling up and down Kingsland Road, and over the fair. Saturday nights we were loaded and round about twelve o'clock we would make for the coffee-stall which was on the corner of Ridley Road, next to Woolworths'. There would always be a crowd round the stall and the speciality would be an 'All On'. This was a massive sandwich filled with everything but the kitchen sink: sausage, tomato, egg, watercress, beetroot and everything else that could be crammed into it. To devour one of these jumbos was a two-handed operation. The sandwich was 1/6d and the tea 3d. A grand sum of 1/9d, a bit expensive but well worth it. Everyone would be shouting their orders:

'Two All Ons, Joe!'

'Four teas and six All Ons, Joe!'

Joe had to work full pelt on Saturday nights when the pubs turned out. It was a marvel to see this man at work, sausages frying away in one pan, bacon in another, beetroot to be cut, bread to be buttered and money to be taken. His assistant lightened the burden by making the tea. And did he have to move! Slopping the milk in the cups, then the sugar, almost throwing the cups into the counter, the tea spilling over it. You'd place your money on the tea-soaked counter and it was promptly picked up by Joe before someone else did it for him. The coins were soaked in tea.

You would stand there listening to the latest jokes, coming from the young and elderly, really enjoying your meal, unless of course Oswald Mosley's fascist party was there, just a few yards up the road, spewing out their party doctrine, and that would be enough to make anyone sick.

But this is where our enjoyment used to be, this was our world and this is one part of my life I can look back on with nostalgia, not a care in the world. No real worries or problems for us, and if we had them, I don't suppose we would have realised them anyway. We were too young to realise anything.

Ginger Pearson was the leader of the boys who frequented the fairground. He was an expert at breaking into fruit machines. There used to be an amusement arcade in Kingsland Road, where Burton's now stands. The proprietor would always be sitting in an armchair at the back of the arcade. If you wanted change you had to go to him to get it. He seemed a listless type of man, but his listlessness found a quick cure when he saw how often Ginger was winning. Ginger just could not lose on this certain pintable. What he used to do remains a mystery to this day. He would put a penny in and shoot a ball up the table. He would then give the table a sort of bear hug, with his arms pressing underneath. Time and time again the proprietor would have to pay out. And it was this persistent winning by Ginger that got the proprietor on his feet. He would stand a few feet behind Ginger, watching, like a cat watches a mouse, but he could not for the life of him see what Ginger was up to, nor could the boys. The time came when the proprietor decided that he had suffered enough: Ginger was banished from the arcade for ever.

This was only one of his tricks. Another one was this. There used to be a machine over the fair which you looked in and saw a nude show, after inserting a penny. He would tell us boys all to gather round, as though we were looking through the viewer, and while we were engaged in this activity, Ginger would be engaged in another — namely, undoing the lock underneath and collecting the coins. His haul would be spent on fish and chips.

On a Sunday afternoon, if there was any money left, we would go to the Odeon, just off Kingsland Road, or the Classic, on the corner of John Campbell Road, or the Savoy, a little further up Kingsland Road. That is, of course, if we had not been banned from them. If the bar was up to us at all three, then we would have to come off of our territory, and make for the Empress in Mare Street, which is now a Bingo hall.

This last one was a cinema in a million. I think it got blasted during the bombing and had not yet been repaired. Once the film started the lads would start their antics, getting up to go to talk to someone, throwing sweets or anything that was handy at the heads in front. Chopper Moseley's speciality was stink bombs, but on one occasion he had discovered a different version of his usual weapon. This was a bottle filled with a vile-smelling liquid which you just sprinkled on people; much more handy than carrying glass pellets in your pocket, for if someone accidentally, or purposely, bumped against you, then the weapon would automatically be turned on yourself. Anyway, on one occasion he decided to take a back seat, where the more respectable, elderly patrons would sit, out of our way. He managed to get behind a courting couple of about twentyish. Out came Chopper's potion. Taking out the cork with one hand, handkerchief over his mouth with the other, he struck. He let just a trickle fall on the chap's shoulder in front. The couple in front were too engrossed with each other to realise what was happening. Seconds after, the girl's head sprang up from her lover's shoulder and gave him a penetrating look. He turned his head towards her, then it was whisper, whisper, a look round and a fidget in the seats. They decided to settle down again and try to ignore this unfriendly odour, but it was just not ignorable. Their attention was just drawn to it. So they had enough and up they got hoping to find refuge in another seat. But to no avail. They moved three or four times and gave up in defeat, and out they went, oblivious of the liquid on the chap's shoulder, and unaware that this strench would last another couple of hours.

Chopper was reeling in his seat, legs bent up as he lay back in the seat hardly able to draw breath through fits of laughter.

On another occasion at the Empress, during the interval, one of the boys began studying the ceiling.

'Hey,' he said to Ginger. 'That's an unusual type of ceiling, ain't it Ginge, it looks just like the sky.'

He probably hadn't been there before.

'Looks like the sky, you silly daft git – it is the sky!'

The boy looked puzzled at this and looked at Ginger in disbelief. Still puzzled and confused he asked, as if to catch Ginger,

'What happens if it rains, then?'

Ginger was getting impatient at this, for he was the boss and he knew everything.

'Oh,' said Ginger, 'you are a curous little thing, ain't you. Well, when it rains see, you collect your umbrella at the bleedin' door, right?'

If you were a newcomer to this cinema, you had to be careful where you sat and how you sat. You would see people edging down the row, with eyes on the screen, putting their hands behind them to pull the seat down, only to discover that there wasn't a seat. When you did get a seat, you would find yourself sinking deeper and deeper into it; there was a great hole right in the middle. You would have to get up very carefully because the springs might have come through the worn material and worked themselves into the seat of your trousers. As you stood erect, the seat would spring up and your arse would be trapped. You would then have to be rescued by one of the boys, but not until they had had a good laugh at your predicament. You would be sure never to get so carried away with the film and make the foolish mistake of resting your chin in your hand and leaning on one of the arms – there might not be any arm there and you would finish up leaning on the person next to you. This would be most embarrassing if the one next to you happened to be a girl, or even worse, some old dear.

At that time the stars would be Burt Lancaster and Tony Curtis a star whose hair style the boys would copy. This style would be called a D.A., short for District Attorney, officially that is, unofficially it was given the name of 'duck's arse' by the boys, for the simple reason that the hair each side of the head would be swept back and meet at the back of the head, overlapping like duck's wings.

There was a film out called 'The African Queen'. I saw this more times than I can remember, not because I liked it so much, but the fact was that my mate's mother worked at the Ritz at Clapton Pond, and we used to get in free. This is how I met my wife for she

worked in the cinema also. And so that I could get more friendly
with her, it was 'The African Queen' the whole week through for
me and my mate Bert. Bert was glad when the week was over.

'Oh, no, Ron,' he would moan. 'Not again tonight please. I'm
bleeding dreaming about the African Queen.'

But he saw my intentions. He could see it wasn't the African
Queen I was interested in. Poor old Bert.

We used to go to a youth club in Stoke Newington Church
Street. I was the one who discovered this club. I happened to pick up
with this little girl Rita; she was a very nice type of girl, and she
took me to her club.

'Well,' I said, 'I'll tell the boys about this and we'll have a good
old time here.'

By the look on her face I could tell she didn't like this idea, but
I told them just the same. She didn't like me going with this lot.
They may have seemed rough and rowdy but underneath they were
real genuine kids. If some of us had money and the others didn't,
then we'd share the money out, no matter whether it was for
pictures, the arcade or anything else. None of us had anything or
went anywhere without the other. If there was about eight of us, and
we went in the fish shop and found we had only enough for four
bags of chips then we would get four and share them out. We would
be classed as ruffians perhaps by others, but these boys were what
you'd call real mates. We'd fight each other it's true. Ginger might
put one on you for paying too much attention to his bird, but then
it was over and done with. We'd all be pals again.

Well, anyway, to get back to the club. There would be a hall with
the record player going. The dances then were the Jive, the Creep and
the Boogie. Not much different to what the kids do today, only then
you had to learn the steps; today they seem to make them up as they
go along, and I don't think this is a bad thing — it gives the youngsters
more freedom of expression.

There was also a smaller hall off from the main hall, in which there
was a piano. I would go in there to have a go on it. I was not in there
long before all the lads and girls were in.

'Go on, Ron, go on, In the Mood!' This was one of Glenn Miller's
big hits. But I used to love boogie music, although I could never pick
up the intricate melodies, and the bass playing independently of the
right hand was most difficult. So what I did was to play a three note
bass and the melody I would make up with my right hand as I went
along. And they loved it. But getting over my difficulties in this way,

I could not help feeling that I was cheating them. But they were happy and so was I.

In about 1948, conscription into the army became compulsory for boys of eighteen. I escaped this ordeal by the skin of my teeth by being Grade 3. I think my father had something to do with this, for I still have my attendance card and on the back it says, 'If you have any serious illness, or if your health has deteriorated in any way, you must inform your local Labour Exchange'. I think my father went to the Labour Exchange and told them about my asthma, for when I had a tiff with him, some time after my exemption, he said,

'Just think why it was you got out of the army.' I don't think the army would have liked me very much, for I don't think I could take an order and go to it just like a machine, without thinking whether the order was a good or bad one first. No, I don't think I would have gone down very well at all. So after the I.Q. test, chest and limbs examination, and the usual Cough, Cough, I was a free man.

And this was really the breaking up of the gang; there was only two or three of us left now. We were a bit older and had become a little more tame. We courted and before you could say Jack Robisnon, we were married men. What a pity the way this little group had broken up. No more fairground meetings, no more All Ons, no more pranks. This was it: we now had to become men, and face all life's problems, as unequipped as we were, and bring up our families and provide for them.

I wonder how many youngsters today, who at seventeen have all the advantages of this modern age, enjoy themselves as much as we did. And I wonder if they are as happy as we were then. We can only hope that they are.

# 6

I will never forget the poor fellow I saw in my last polishing job.
He was about twenty and deaf and dumb. The men used to make fun
of this poor chap and tease him all the time. He was a labourer. The
men harassed him so much that he would sit alone behind one of the
wardrobes during our meal breaks. I felt really sorry for this poor
fellow. He would be laughed at, kicked and played tricks on. I would
have tried to make a friend of him and show him a bit of kindness,
but if I had done this I would have been for it also.

I thought, well it's my last week anyway, and I tried to make
friends with this fellow. During the tea break I left the circle of men
who were telling jokes and did not notice my departure. I made my
way round the back of the wardrobe. He was sitting there, head
bowed, sandwiches in his lap and his cup of tea on the floor at his
side. He was sitting on a pile of sacks. I gradually worked my way
round so that I approached him from the front – he may have
panicked if he saw me coming from behind, thinking I was going to
do something to him. He saw me coming towards him. He stopped
chewing. I was about fifteen feet away from him. I grabbed a drawer
to sit on and as I did so he sat up stiffly, alert. I picked up my tea
and before I took a sip I smiled at him. He looked belligerently
towards me. As the cup left my mouth I frowned at him and pointed
to the cup of tea I had just tasted, conveying to him what I thought
of it. He just stared at me like a frightened animal and with that he
raised himself and walked away.

I persevered all week like this with him; every meal break I would
try to make contact with him, and he seemed to be getting angrier
with my persistence. Friday arrived at last, my last day in the polishing
game. At dinner time I had bought a packet of sweets. We had just got
up ready to start work. I was at my bench. I thought, I'll try offering
him a sweet. He was moving some 'robes' into the polishing shop at
the time and saw me coming. I went straight towards him, holding
my bag out. He looked at the bag suspiciously. He looked at me.

46

Suddenly he threw out a right that missed my face by inches. We stood looking at each other straight in the eyes. In his eyes I read bewilderment and fear, sadness and loneliness. This is what the world had done to this poor man.

I often wonder what he would have been like had he been brought up in a more tender and understanding environment, instead of having to work among hard men who lived hard lives going on from generation to generation. I am not saying by any means that all the working class are hard and mean people, but there are those among us who have had a hard childhood as well as a hard adulthood, in an environment where to show any love or feeling for humanity is ridiculed, and the person is reckoned as soft.

It was six o'clock, time to knock off. I was the only one to put on my coat, the rest were working overtime that night. I said cheerio to all the men. As I made for the door the wardrobes were on my right, and as I passed them I looked round – why I don't know – but but there was the mute fellow looking at me, one hand resting against a robe. I turned to make for the door and then heard a sound like 'Hu . . . hu . . . ' I then stopped and just then I felt a hand on my shoulder. I turned – yes it was him actually touching me. We looked at each other, in his eyes I could read thanks.

I then wished I had stayed on, but I was by this time sick of the polishing trade, just one more trade where you were unable to put all your skill into the job and make it absolutely perfect, as it should be. Everything was rush, rush, rush, get it out as quickly as possible – that is all they required.

While in the polishing game I went from one job to another, working in dingy little cellars, almost in complete darkness, and with toilet facilities that were indescribable. And yet compared with the conditions of the working people at the beginning of the nineteenth century, I suppose we all had a lot to be thankful for.

I had now left the french polishing, for I began to realise how harmful this trade was for my condition. I had applied for a job as a bread-roundsman at Prices Bread Company in Leswin Road, Stoke Newington. I thought being in the open air would be better for me.

Although horses and carts were well out of date, this firm still had a number of them as well as petrol motors at their Leswin Road depot in Stoke Newington. I was sent out with an inspector to learn the round and how to do the book. I arrived about six in the morning, and I reported to the dispatch office, where the inspector was waiting for me.

'Morning, son,' he said. 'You fit?'

'Yes,' I replied.

'Well then, we'll get the horse.'

I thought, what a great experience it will be to drive a horse and cart. We entered the stables, and as we moved along on each side of us were the horses' hind legs. The inspector could see that I was a little nervous as we proceeded down the narrow path.

'What's the matter son, frightened of being kicked?'

'Well, yes, I am rather.'

'Don't worry about that, mate, what you've gotta watch is that they don't shits on you, that's all. What's yer name?'

'Ron.'

'Mine's Charlie. Right, this is our horse, he's Charlie an' all.'

He was a beautiful horse with a chestnut brown coat, and as quiet as a mouse. I seemed to take to him right away.

'Well, go inside the stall then and get him out,' said two-legged Charlie.

For some unknown reason I was not a bit afraid of getting right up to him.

'Mind he don't tread on yer feet,' two-legged Charlie said, 'cause if he does yer won't move him, cause he don't know he's on 'em, yer see, ha, ha, ha.'

I led him out to the cart and Charlie showed me how to harness a horse, which I found quite difficult at first, but I soon got the hang of it after a few tries. We went and had breakfast in the cafe and then started the round.

'Well,' Charlie said, 'your round will be Hoxton. Now keep your eyes open where we are going.'

He showed me how to do the book and how to put a nosebag on.

'Right, now comes the most important part of all. You're gonna get plenty of 'knockers' round 'ere. They'll come out looking so pitiful, they'll say something like, "Just let me have one more loaf and some biscuits, and I promise to pay you for sure on Saturday, and me old man will be out of prison soon and then I can clear you right up then." Or it might be, "Me 'usbands sick and been home for months now, after falling off that scaffold at work." But I tell you son, don't have none of it. I'm not saying they're not telling the truth mind, because I know most of 'em are, but if you let them run up big bills for months on end you will never get your money.'

'And then?' I said.

48

'And then you'll have me after you,' said Charlie, 'because the old man's after me. As you go on you'll know who you can trust and who you can't. If you get a new customer don't let her have a lot of stuff at first, until you know what sort of payer she is.'

'But suppose she is a good customer and has a lot of stuff and always pays well and then her husband falls sick, or ends up in clink, and she can't pay as well as she did?' I asked.

'Well if you know her husband aint working, and she says she can't pay this week, then let her see that you are most annoyed, and tell her that you are losing commission over it – that might make her try a little harder to pay you next week. Once she is two weeks in arrears, drop her, don't give her anymore stuff until she's given you a good bit off. Don't have none of that hard luck stuff from anyone, right?'

'But it doesn't seem right to treat a poor woman like that, she might be desperate for bread for her kids – who knows, that might be all she can give them.'

'Now look 'ere!' he shouted. 'If you're gonna think like that bleeding way, don't start the job, become a bleeding monk or something, because you just can't think like that in this world.'

'Is anyone going to look after your wife and kids if you're sick or anything?'

'No, I don't suppose anyone will,' he said.

'Well there you are then. To be like this towards each other can't be right then, can it?'

'No mate, it aint right but that's life, aint it?'

'Yes that is life,' I said, 'but we're the only ones that can change it.

'Yes, well I've got other things on my mind so I'll leave that for you to think about.'

After two or three weeks I was out on my own. I grew very fond of my horse, Charlie, and I would take a carrot or some sugar into his stable after we had done our day's work. I had many an arguement with the stable foreman for refusing to take him out with a sore on his back, where his collar rubbed.

Charlie would stop at the same greengrocer's shop everyday on his own accord, to receive his carrot. I would never force his pace, no matter how late I was. If he wanted to walk, he walked, if he wanted to trot, he trotted, if he wanted to run – which was not very often – he ran. He knew my voice well, and he knew every inch of the round. If I met one of my customers as I came out of the cafe, or if I happened to be behind the cart, he would recognise my voice and his head would turn completely round so that he could see me. He was such a quiet horse, and very safe with children.

When I used to go into the flats and the kids were on their holidays, they would crowd round Charlie and ask me for a ride on his back. How could I refuse these kids, some of whom had never seen the seaside, who had never seen real farm animals, only in their school books? Despite them making a nuisance of themselves round the cart, I used to give one or two of them a ride on Charlie's back. With all these kids around me, I had to keep an eye on my cakes in the back of the cart, or it was possible that I would be cleared right out of cakes before I left the flats. I used to employ an older boy to guard the van for me when the children were away from school, and I would pay him one shilling before I left the flats. He would also help himself while I was gone, but I said nothing to him about this; I thought it better to suffer the loss of a few cakes to this boy than to lose a cart load.

I accumulated many bad debts on my books; I was just unable to refuse these poor women bread. I used to try to get as much from them as possible, but I could never threaten them with any of the things that Charlie the inspector told me. Some of them tried to take liberties with me but when I saw this I let them know I wasn't having any. How could I refuse bread to the woman who had lost a fiver just before I called on the Saturday, or the woman who was three weeks behind in the rent because she had been ill and her husband had had to stay at home and look after her? Or the young girl whose husband had left her with three children to look after, wives whose husbands had been made redundant, and many other cases? How in the name of humanity could I refuse these people who through no fault of their own were in poverty, the poverty that I was to experience after I was married?

'The earth is the Lord's and the fullness thereof.' If this is so, all this abundance of the earth, the fruit and vegetables, minerals and all the rest of the natural wealth, why in the name of almighty god do people have to be in poverty? What faith can one have in the human race, when those living in the lap of luxury can live just round the corner from those in poverty, and can pass by with complete indifference. What sort of generation is this, a generation conditioned to accept these two extremes of poverty, a generation striving to possess more than the other. A brother is not a brother, only by name, in reality he is an opponent, a threat to your way of life. Need we look any further for the cause of mental illness, family fighting and unhappiness?

What sort of place is this, when a family lives in damp housing, with restricted space, three or four to a bedroom, people who, even in this day and age of so-called 'affluence', are unable to afford a holiday and many other things besides? And the philosophy of these people is, 'Ah well, we could be worse off I suppose.' And then I read of a financier living in a luxury hotel who has been relieved of ninety thousand pounds in jewellery by bandits, consisting of cuff-links and tie-pins, unnecessary trivialities. This when children must go without. God, when are you going to alter these social injustices? When?

After letting a number of bills run up, an inspector was sent out with me as a sort of bogey man to get what he could out of the debtors. He did not get much. He finished the round saying,

'Well, you can't get blood out of a stone.'

But these people were not like stone, they would help each other like most people wouldn't dream of doing. They were not made of stone; they just didn't have the money.

I can remember Grannie Gullis telling me about her young days when she would go to work with no breakfast, no dinner, nothing inside her until she got home at night from work. This was in the 1900's. She told me that at times she would pass out with hunger, the girls got so used to it that it was no longer a shock to them to see her drop to the floor of the factory. They thought she had an illness; little did they know that this was malnutrition. She has had to have many operations over this, and now has very little stomach left, but still she goes on, over eighty-three years of age. 'Poverty', she says, 'people today don't know what it is.'

I was now about eighteen. I had met my wife, Dolly, at the Ritz picture house at Clapton Pond. We courted about a year or so and then she fell pregnant. At eighteen she had lost both her parents, she was completely alone in the world, and although I had both parents, I felt completely the same. Whether we loved each other I don't know. At such a young age, with myself not really knowing about love, we could not possibly have known. We had sex and perhaps thought that that was love. She had known love, and perhaps now being alone she needed someone to love and be loved by. I knew nothing of love, forgiveness, thoughtfulness, tenderness. It seems, when I look back, that all these many desirable traits were completely lacking in me.

So we had to get married. We had about eighty pounds between us, which wasn't bad at that time. We had to live with my parents, but we did have a room to ourselves. We got married in West Hackney Church, Amhurst Road. And what a wedding that was. We had spent our money on a second-hand, three-piece which was green. I can still hear my mother saying,

'Green, well it's nice, but green, well you know what they say about green, don't you? Very unlucky they say.'

We bought curtains, a small carpet and other odds and ends, so now we were almost skint.

I think about a dozen people came to the church, on foot of course; we could afford no fancy trappings like cars, and very little drink. No wedding gown for Dolly, no photos – nobody thought of bringing a camera along – and this was the way we got married. We went back home where a little fat man pummelled the worn out piano which sounded as though it was in its last death throes. What drink there was had been handed round to our dozen or so guests, before departing for the West End for our slap up meal.

We walked along Oxford Street until we came to Selfridges.

'Oh look at those curtains, Ron,' my wife said, 'ain't they beautiful?'

'Yes,' I said, 'they are.'

'I'd like them – they'd go lovely with our three piece.' (Which by the way, cost us twenty pounds).

Then I saw the price: Five pounds a yard.

'Come on,' I said. 'They're not for the likes of us'.

We walked around for a couple of hours. We saw wedding dresses at £200, fur coats, jewellery, all at fantastic prices.

'Judging by these prices,' I said, 'God knows what they're going to charge us for this meal.'

The West End of London – it's another world – people living in a way that we could never dream or imagine. This to me was not London, not my London. Not the warm, neighbourly London of the East End. This was a new land of cold, hard buildings, with a cold, hard type of people, with a different accent, with a different sense of humour, if any. No, I disliked the West End, you could feel its coldness and indifference all around you. There was something lacking in spite of its culture and its luxury and its tradition. We had our meal and I was glad to get back to my native land.

So our married life began in one room, at 40 Brooke Road. After six months Doll had to pack up work, then we began to feel the pinch. What with our living money, and things to get for the coming baby, things were very tight indeed.

The room, although quite big, would continually be in a jumble, and what with our financial position, and myself coming home from work tired, the arguments started, arguments that led to fights between us. It was now I felt the drawback of being an asthmatic. I had frequent colds, and after having one week off work it would take weeks to recover my losses and just after I had got myself straight, I would be sick again. When this happened I had to quickly grab the next job so as to keep my head above water. I would not consider whether or not the job suited me, or whether it would be detrimental to my health. As long as it was a job, it suited me.

Then the day came when our daughter was brought to our one room, which we called home. It was a marvellous feeling indeed, and one of the happiest moments of our life, to have our own baby. Money was short and, as much as I disliked it, Lesley our daughter was put in the nursery as soon as she was old enough. Dolly's money was a great help, but my continual sickness reduced our income quite a bit at the end of the year. And this is where my musical talent came in.

I answered an advert in the paper for a pub pianist. I had never played the piano in a pub in all my life, but I thought, well I am pretty good, I might get by. My financial position spurred me on. Fifteen shillings a night, Friday, Saturday and Sunday, that was another two pounds, five a week. So after my week's work. I would do this pub work at the weekends. This went on for a good number of years, but this left Dolly at home on her own for many a weekend.

No wonder our marriage gradually got worse and worse. Every week I would say, "O.K. I'll give it a rest this week', but when it came round to it I was there at the pub as usual. How we stuck the life, I don't know. We both didn't like pubs too much, and this was one of the reasons why Dolly wouldn't come with me. We missed many Christmases together with our baby, and many New Year's Eves too. All so we could pay our way and not have to claim on the Unemployment Assistance Board (U.A.B.) now the Social Security.

Some nights I would be playing, and feeling very depressed, and no one would be paying much attention to the piano. I would be looking at the customers drinking with their wives and their friends, and I would think, if I didn't have to do this, Doll and I could be out together, or, what we liked best, sitting together at home listening to the wireless, or perhaps I would be pottering about doing something; we liked the quiet life. These feelings and thoughts made me even more depressed; I had to dismiss them as soon as I found myself dwelling on them. If it wasn't for poor wages and this bloody asthma, I wouldn't be here playing this bloody heap of rubbish they call a piano. Perhaps a drunk would come up, 'Come on, son, I wanna shing Nellie Dean.' They would lay all over you, stinking of sweat and beer, often unwashed and unshaven, coming in straight from work in their dirty overalls.

At the weekend the pub would be filled with its usual fight-happy characters. I remember one in particular who got his eye gouged out with an umbrella. Then there was a chap from Scotland who thought he would see how much damage he could do to the pub premises in the shortest possible time. By the time he had almost finished the pub was minus all its windows, the juke-box was a write-off and there was hardly a drinking glass left. Before he could get started on the counter itself, the police arrived.

This was the atmosphere I had to endure for many years, but fortunately it did come to an end, but not before its time. Some of the pubs in the East End have them all: queers, lesbians, vagrants, crooks, the lot. The continual playing for money, and in this sort of atmosphere, made me wish never to see a piano again. So by earning money for my talent, I nearly killed the joy of being able to play an instrument. I would never play for money ever again.

Well by the time the bread round was getting me down, what with the stairs and the weather. I had to pack it up. I then started a job lorry-driving. I know now that driving wasn't for me — and still isn't — but that's the way life is for many people; there are hundreds of thousands in the wrong job.

The thought of being an artist still haunts me. I often think of taking it up, but work and domestic committments don't seem to allow it. The things I would like to do are endless and I'm sure I'm not on my own in this: painting, music, reading, writing, photography, tape-recording, boating, swimming, tennis, to mention only a few. But how many people have the time, and also the energy after a week's work? And if they do have the energy, where do they get the money that most of these enjoyments cost?

Things were very tight at this time. We began to argue, often about money, and we vented our frustrations out on each other with biting words we didn't really mean. We didn't realise at the time that it was not us but the conditions of living in one room. My father used to get annoyed when Dollie boiled the nappies in the saucepan in the kitchen, and he would tell my mother and my mother would tell Doll. So she would have to leave them and when I came home I would be mad at seeing this heap of napkins in the room where we and the baby had to sleep. Another big row was caused when Dollie, after finishing the ironing in our room, had no cupboard to put the hot iron away, so she left it by the fireplace on the floor. She turned her back for a few seconds and then heard the baby scream out. Lesley had crawled to the fireplace and had fell on the iron, badly burning her arm. She still has the scar today; I am thankful it wasn't her face.

Because I was weak in health, the monotony of work would tire me very quickly and by the time I got home I was far from being congenial. But how was we to know the cause? At school we were taught nothing of psychology, nothing of how a person should know himself, his bad characteristics as well as his good ones, and how to suppress the one and develop the other. So what happens? A youngster is influenced by what goes on around him, and what goes on around many working class children is far from beneficial. He picks up the characteristics of violence: if a person won't do as you say, well then use violence: don't talk over a thing quietly, shout and brawl. The parents who show these characteristics are not to blame in themselves, for they have learnt the same in their family. Generation after generation are lacking in education, I mean a good education, not just the three R's. Put these things together with bad housing, bad wages and you must get a good percentage of criminals; fortunately, there are many who survive this type of environment.

Eventually we had a letter from the housing people to go and view a house at Southwold Road. The rent was £3.10.0. per week. The housing department, having had a certificate from my doctor telling them of my asthma, considered this flat ideal for my family. The flat was on the top floor, eight flights of stairs, no lift. This nineteenth century block that reminded one of a prison was built on the fair plains of the Marshes. The stairs were ideal for breathing exercises, and the damp mist that came up night and morning was ideal for chest sufferers.

I was unable to go with Doll and my mother to view the flat; I could not afford to lose the money. When I got in on the evening, they both told me how nice it was. Understandably, to Doll it was marvellous, plenty of room in the kitchen, her own kitchen at that, our own bedroom, living room, and a bedroom for baby as well as a bath. How could we refuse such a place after one room? The only thing was we were not experienced enough to reckon on dampness and mildew. We didn't give the stairs a thought, or the fact that we were at the bottom of a steep hill and had a walk of about a quarter of a mile to the main road. But anyhow, we rushed at it.

We moved in with what little possessions we had, and were full of optimism about getting a lot of new furniture, especially a new bedroom suite, an item that we still haven't been able to afford even at the time of writing this book. The working class are fed this crap about saving; nobody could have saved more than me. I had to save to allow for my periods of sickness. It is true that saving can be a great help, but no one in the working class ever became or ever will become rich by it, unless, of course, they are able to put away about two hundred pounds a week into a building society, or in stocks and shares, then they will become rich for doing nothing.

# 7

In the course of a couple of years I must have got through about twenty jobs. One such job was typical: working for a laundry. What with the stairs when delivering, and the dampness in the laundry, I had to have considerable time off. The foreman didn't take to this kindly and was most hostile, repeating the same old phrase that all businessmen use as their favourite standby: 'We've got a business to run, we're very sorry, but we've got a business to run'. Yes, they are sorry, sorry about loss of profits, not the person.

I then started a job for a timber firm. The foreman seemed quite a nice fellow.

'Handled timber before?' he said.

'Yes,' I replied. Lie number one.

'Are you fit to do this work?'

'Yes,' Lie number two.

'Have you handled a three-tonner before?'

'Yes I have.' Lie number three.

'O.K. Start Monday.'

I shall never forget that job, for it was here that I met the greatest friend I have ever had. It was a time when West Indian immigration was at its highest. I had had no dealings with the people, who I knew as blacks or wogs or coons.

I had just started. I was loading my lorry with timber and I didn't have a clue how to stack it so that it would not fall off the lorry on the journey. I had got about half the load on when this giant of a West Indian fellow came up to me.

'Well, that doesn't look too good, you know. Look, I'll show you.'

He helped me put the other half on, which was now stacked better than the first half.

'Well,' he said. 'It should hold until you get to Greys if you take it steady.'

I thanked him for his help. I then had to tie my load up and this was something else I didn't have a clue about. I hesitated until my helper was out of the way, for the reason that in the transport game if you do not tie the load to the accepted way, the way that all drivers do, then it stands out a mile that you're not a lorry driver.

So satisfied that my dark friend was nowhere about, I threw the rope over the load, and tried to tie this special knot — with no success. So intent was I in my task that I did not notice this black fellow coming.

'You having trouble, mister?'

'Er, no, it's all right.'

'I don't think you've got it there, you know,' he said. 'Let me try it.'

In no time the load was tied. He looked down at me with a slight grin.

'Don't worry man, I won't say nothing. I'll help you till you know how to load and tie.'

Why was it that with a number of white labourers in that yard, it was a black fellow who had to come and help me. This taught me that race is nothing — it is individuals that matter. You take no notice of what you hear about people; you meet them and judge them for yourself.

Well, in spite of the help I was given, my whole load came off half way to Greys, and I had to load the lot myself. Not having driven a large vehicle before, the journey was none too smooth, but I managed to deliver the load and get back to London, but not before demolishing a brick wall while reversing, which I heard nothing about, and then reversing into a jallopy whilst reversing back into the timber yard. When you are not used to reversing a large vehicle, you can do considerable damage: you have to lean out of the door, and this gives you a feeling that you are going to fall out any minute. Anyhow, I managed to overcome my difficulties and was able to keep the job.

One summer dinner time as I drove into the yard, all the labourers were sitting round the coloured chap who had helped me to load up. Some were listening to him, some were reading and some were making witty remarks and laughing and shouting. What's going on, I thought. I got out of my cab and joined the rest with my sandwiches. One sawdust-laden fellow shouted at the black fellow,

'Who is this bloke Jesus, then?'

'Jesus paid the price of sin for us all,' came the answer from the black fellow.

'Here,' shouted the heckler, 'Do you think he could pay the

price of a pair of shoes for us, only mine are gone right through?'

This caused the listeners to go into ecstasies of laughter.

'Believe me brother, your soul is in a much worse state than your shoes. You can buy new shoes, yes, but can you buy a new soul?'

'That's good that is!' shouted the heckler. 'New shoes? Not down Petticoat Lane you don't. Bleedin' second-hand, that's what!'

'You should be thankful for what you have,' said the black fellow.

'Oh, yes,' came the reply. 'Be thankful that you work all bleedin' year and can't afford a bleedin' holiday, or a new suit, or give your kids the things they need, like a good education, and housing, and fruit and milk, and all the rest. Be bleedin' thankful, he says!'

'All right, all right!' shouted some of the men. 'Don't start getting serious.'

Well, I thought, this fellow is a Christian. Although I had never been a church-goer, I was always drawn to religion for some reason or other. Anyway, it was time to start work again and he stood up, saying, 'Come unto me all ye that labour and are heavy-laden and I will give you rest,' raising his hands to emphasise these words. Up they all got with one of the men saying something about 'I've had all the rest I need.'

As time went on I began to get to know this religious fellow more. It happened that I asked him what he did with himself at the weekends. He told me he went to church, and asked me along with him. We met on the Sunday night and off we went to Richmond Road, Dalston Methodist Church. This church had lent a hall to another church called The Church of God in Christ. This was the church we were going to. As I went in I was confronted with a mass of worshippers, all black. We found a seat in the middle of the hall, mine being the only white face among the lot. At first for some reason I felt a little, well I don't know, perhaps you could say scared, but of what I really couldn't say: it may have been of the religious atmosphere, or perhaps being amongst people I wasn't used to.

In time I came to realise as I got to know these people that my fears were not justified, for these people turned out to be the most friendly, most genuine, most loving people I had ever met. I now realise, in these latter days (1973), how fortunate I have been to meet and keep as friends these wonderful West Indian Christians. There was something they had that others didn't; one could sense a sort of peace and contentment about them, that others didn't seem to have, and for sure that thing was faith in God.

We sat there together while some of the congregation stood up one by one and gave their testimony of how the Lord had helped them through the week and so on. After this came some negro spirituals. These songs certainly have been given the right name, Negro Spiritual, for these songs are full of meaning and sincerity, many of them going back to the times of slavery. And when you are among these people singing these wonderful songs, one's life is complete, all your fears, tensions and cares dissolve and fade away. To me this was the experience of a lifetime: never before had I seen a church with this wonderful atmosphere. Mothers with children were allowed to let their children walk around if they became restless, a baby might cry out while some one was speaking, or while the elder was giving the evening sermon; no one would be at all disturbed by these distractions whatsoever.

Elder Marsh was the minister of this particular church, and a very sincere man he was. So overcome at times with his love of God, the tears would roll down his cheeks as he proclaimed the word of God, making no attempt at all to conceal his tears. He once said, why be ashamed to cry when you know what you were and you know how God has changed you, through faith in him. This way this man spoke, his sincerity, and feeling, caused me to feel very much ashamed of myself, and who of us has never felt this.

After going with the black fellow a few times, we grew very fond of each other and we now called each other brother: he was my brother Derek, or Dixon, and I was brother Ronnie. And we were brothers in the true sense of the word, although no two brothers could look less alike, he being a dark nut brown, and six feet tall, and myself being of sallow complexion, standing at five foot four. In our appearance we were different, but in our hearts we were twins.

After about three weeks of going to church, I felt something happening inside me. It was one Wednesday evening when Elder Marsh gave the evening message which was about friendship, telling us that Jesus was the truest friend that a person could have. A chorus was sung, a chorus I shall never forget as long as I live.

> I've wandered far away from God,
> Now I'm coming home,
> The path of sin too long I've trod,
> Now I'm coming home.

Open wide thy arms of love,
Lord, I'm coming home.

I arose from my seat. I was the first to go forward, something
seemed to take hold of me, urging me towards the altar. I was
oblivious to the people around me, all I knew was that I had to go
forward. I knelt at the altar; a feeling of such peace and tranquility
coming over me, a feeling I had never experienced before. Elder
Marsh prayed over me. I went back to my seat feeling that something had changed within me. On taking my seat I began to sob, my
head in my hands. Why this came over me I do not know, but now I
was a Christian. I changed completely for the good.

I would study my bible and testify in church and even give the
evening message, something I never thought I was capable of doing.
But when you feel so deeply about something the words seem to
come so easily. But that was in 1957 and now I find myself unable
to accept the Christian faith entirely, particularly the doctrine that
all non-believers will be damned to eternal destruction. I have met
many people who are full of goodness and kind deeds, who really
feel for humanity but are not Christians. They may be Jews, Buddhists
or what have you, but because they are not Christians they will be
condemned; this I cannot accept at any price.

Brother Derek has been the truest friend I have ever had. And I
consider myself fortunate to have met such a man and when I say
a man that is just what I mean, a true man if ever I saw one. He
used to tell me, 'I don't have any enemies, Brother Ron, only
friends.' He is the truest and closest to being a Christian than many
so-called Christians claim to be. To me he is a blood brother.

# 8

By 1964 I had gone through about sixteen jobs, being sacked for losing time or because the job was too much for my health. I had also put in for an industrial training course at the labour exchange and what a performance that was: you would have thought I had asked for the Crown Jewels. I told the board, which consisted of middle-class businessmen who hadn't a clue, what it was to be at the mercy of those who could employ you or sack you, take you on if it was profitable to them or tell you that the vacancy was filled if it was not. What do I mean by profitable? Why, being fit of course. Never mind about the welfare of the person, or what it will do to him or her physically and mentally being unemployed. Profit is the motive of every business. Did I hear something said about the welfare state, and firms having to take on so many disabled, and if they do it is looked on as a favour. What I am saying I know to be true.

I will tell you a little story. One day I was sent from the disabled department to a firm in Stoke Newington as a driver to a traveller. After telling him of my past experience at driving, he seemed most eager to start me. Until I mentioned that I had asthma. He didn't know how to wriggle out of this one.

'Well,' he said, 'well, er em, you know that you will have to be away quite a lot, and you might get sick while you are on the road?'

Here it comes, I thought.

'Well,' I said, 'I have tablets to get me over. It's not often that I get so bad that I couldn't get home in a car.'

'Well I don't think it would suit you really,' he said.

'But you were so keen just a minute ago?'

'No, son, I don't think it would suit you. Of course I am thinking of you.'

I thought, if you really are thinking of me, give me the damned job so I can pay my rent and feed my kid properly. But no, he was thinking of me. That is a matter of opinion.

There are many people who go to work who are disabled, but nobody pays them any attention. Why? Because their disability cannot be seen; they may have migraine, asthma, rheumatism, nervous disorders, etc. Some of these people have no help with regards to pensions. If they reveal their disability to a boss when applying for a job excuses are made and the person is turned away. So you apply for a job and don't reveal your physical or mental condition. After you have had frequent absenteeism, the boss then knows what you are suffering from. You are not sacked at once in a direct way, but you have been marked for the push. You are harassed by the foreman and faults are found with your work. Eventually you break and have to pack up. But to tell you a direct 'No' wouldn't be nice, would it?

I can tell you that what I am writing is absolutely true, this isn't something I've read out of a book, or something I've been taught at university. It is something I've learned first hand by experience. Bosses can sack or take on who they please, when they please and if they please, and it's the small firms who are the worst. The people who have this done to them have no organisation to turn to, and if the firm isn't a closed shop nothing can be done anyway.

So after being sacked, back on the labour you go. They know you by name as soon as you walk in. There you remain for about six months. Suddenly, hurrah! They've found you a job. You are registered disabled. It's a van job delivering laundry. Of course there will be a lot of stairs to climb, and the heat and steam at the laundry will not do your asthma any good. You are then told that the job is not being forced on you, you don't have to take it. What a laugh this one is. In those days I was getting about six pounds a week assistance.

Your kids' shoes are down. There's no coal. You've had enough of tea and toast and skimping and scraping and being called on without warning by the N.A.B. officer. What a laugh: you are not forced to take it.

So the next thing is the interview with the laundry manager. He looks a fit, healthy man.

'Er, how is it that you've been out of work for six months, then?'

'Well, I couldn't get any work.'

'What, you mean to say that you've been on the labour all that time?'

He's thinking you've been in prison. You can't possibly tell them you're an asthmatic, because that would be the end of it. You feel like giving him a mouthful for the unspoken insult you have just received. You bear this humiliation and you get the job. You're all right again for another three or four months and that's how you go on. Isn't freedom wonderful? It's a tribute to these people with their conditions that they keep out of prison like they do.

One child we had, just one. Afraid to have any more in case we could not give them the things in life that they need. I had high hopes for my daughter, but lack of funds would not allow her a good education. And that was with only one child.

Well the labour exchange refused my request to be a cab driver.

'Why do you want to be a cab driver, Mr Barnes?' came a shaky voice from behind a pair of steel-framed glasses, his head down slightly revealing the whole of his bald pink head.

'Well,' I said, 'if I take the "knowledge" of London and become a cabby I will be classed as self-employed. I will then be able to go into work when I feel well enough. Also if I have time off for sickness I cannot be sacked as an employee would. Therefore I would always have a regular job to go back to. My fear of unemploy-ment would be eliminated and would cause a great improvment I am sure in my physical and mental health.

'Em, yes,' said bald head, turning to his two colleagues each side of him. Whisper, whisper, then,

'Well, Mr Barnes, how about the fumes? Yes, the fumes?'

'Well I have been driving all the time, and of course the fumes must affect my condition, but I find that what affects it more is lifting goods on and off of lorries, getting soaked in sweat and then cooling down. This has been a lot of my trouble. The fumes will certainly affect me in the long term, but in the short term I will be in a job where I cannot be sacked, although a garage proprietor can refuse a driver a cab.'

I waited a month. Their reply was that they thought watch-repairing would suit me better. I knew it wouldn't. I was hopeless in school at geometry, figures and measurements. But I attended the training for two months before the instructor came to the con-clusion that I was not cut out for watch-making.

So I was back on the labour again. From 1958 to 1973 I had got through exactly twenty-one jobs, still playing the piano in pubs when things were really tight. It was in 1960, on New Year's Eve, that I became seriously ill. I had been out of work some months, and as much as I would have liked to have stayed at home for the evening, I had to go to the pub. Doll didn't like pubs, but so that we could be together for this night I persuaded her to come with me. It was a good thing that I did. I already had a bad cold, and the weather was absolutely freezing. On the way home the snow was about two feet thick and still falling heavily. My breathing was very bad, my head aching with the cold weather. I held on to Doll for the last three hundred yards to our home? She was literally carrying me along. If she hadn't been with me I would never have made it. The next day I became delirious and the doctor was called and he wanted me to go into hospital, but I refused. But after taking the tablets he gave me I seemed to pull round in a few days.

In about 1968 I decided that I would have to go on the 'knowledge' of London to get my cab-driving licence, and do a part-time job in the meantime. I finally did this because I was not far off forty years of age and getting employment at that age is hard enough for a fit man, let alone a sick one. It took me about two years to get this licence. While I was studying, I took on a job with a driving school in the evenings. I was out all day on my moped learning the routes, and when Doll came home in the evening I was out with the driving school. This went on for two years.

I had tried everything else from selling icecream to hot chestnuts. On the ice-cream job again I was out evenings and weekends, but I thought that once I had my licence I could take things a little easier, which I have done since getting it.

At another time when things were bad I made my own chestnut barrow and can. I would go down to the Arsenal football ground of a Saturday and make a few bob, and sometimes Haringay Stadium. The only thing was that I was not too experienced in keeping the fire under control and on one occasion my whole business went up in flames, so I decided not to continue.

# 9

By this time we had moved from Warwick House, Clapton, to 15 Jackman Street, a dilapidated old house with outside toilet, no bath, and so on. At long last I got my cab-driver's badge and now things began to alter. During this time my father had an heart attack, so we asked him to come and live with us. He refused but some time after had a second heart attack and then he came in with us, but keeping on his other place. It was during this time that I seemed to get to know him more, or so I thought, but he was a very hard man to understand. He seemed the sort of man that had his mind occupied with other things, than in making a family life. He was very good to Lesley, my daughter, when she was very young, but as she got older he seemed to lose interest in her. There were times when we would ask him to come out with us, but he would refuse for he would be happier going out with the children he knew in Jackman Street. Yes, he was very hard to understand and although he seemed rather distant to us, I always respected and loved him.

After he had been with us a few months, the disagreements started. He was out of work, drawing labour money. During this time he had received a little extra labour money, so Doll asked him for a rise in the housekeeping money. He seemed to get most annoyed at this and did not realise how hard it was to keep him and his alsatian dog, Trixie, on three pounds a week. He would also have kids outside his front window and this would annoy the neighbours, with the kids shouting and screaming, but we let it go on, realising that being home all day he got lonely and bored and the kids seemed to cheer him up.

There were many arguments between Doll and my father, about different things, and I was between the two. The five years he was with us was a great strain on all of us. We both loved and respected him but my father was a very strong-willed man and what he said had to be. If he said a thing was black then it was black, even if it might have been a very dark grey. Yes this was my father, small in

66

stature but very strong-willed, able to put his hand and mind to anything. I have even envied at times his versatility in all things. He always thought that his fortune was just round the corner, always dreaming and scheming about how to make a few bob. There is nothing wrong in this I know, but not when it is at the expense of home and family. He would suffer with terrible headaches and depressions at times, and be very miserable, but when he felt all right and in a good mood, he was a very wonderful person, full of wit and humour, and he would have me in fits of laughter at times. I only wish that he would have allowed me to become more involved with him than he did. Like all of us he had his good ways and bad ways, but when it's your father you can see no bad, only good, despite the disagreements and bad feelings at times.

The final conflict we had was when Trixie had to be put down. She had something wrong with her inside. Dad had had her for many years and she had kept him company through his lonely years of living on his own after the divorce. Eventually the dog could not even walk, so she had to be put down. The ambulance came for her during the morning when Doll and I were at work. I'm glad we were, for I couldn't have seen her being taken away for the last time.

When we came home Dad, of course, was very quiet and depressed. Later on in the evening, he said,

'Perhaps I can get another alsatian down the Lane on Sunday morning.'

This really started the ball rolling.

'No, Dad,' said Doll. 'We are not having any more animals. We've got our dog, Flossie, two cats and a guinea pig. No more.'

Dad shouted,

'Oh yes, you've got your cats, you're all right, aint you? Oh yes, you wanted her put down, didn't you — that's what you was waiting for, wasn't it? For her to be put down. You didn't want her here!'

'No Dad, that is not true,' Doll retorted. 'She was with you when you came to live with us, so we took her with you. Anyway, when we move we won't be able to have two dogs, not in a council flat we won't.'

And this is how it went on.

When I got up in the morning, Dad was in the kitchen. He looked at me with tears in his eyes.

'What am I going to do without her?' he said.

'Well you've got Flossie here with you, Dad. You know how she likes you, and how eager she is to go for walks with you. You'll get over it, Dad.'

With that he sat down and started to cry, his head clasped in his hands. This was the first time I had ever seen my father cry. I went to him and held him and leaned over him where he sat and tried to comfort him. How strange life is: when we are children our parents console us in times of stress, and as we get older we have to return the comfort and encouragement they have given us. I really felt for him, but what could I do?

He was a man whose one obsession was to make money, an obsession which was to help towards the break up of his marriage. He was a man who did not seem to value a nice, comfortably furnished home. Our best room, when I was at home with my parents, was always turned into some sort of workshop, and this used to annoy my mother considerably. For, like myself, she always knew the importance of having a nice home to come into after a day's work — but my father did not. Having been poor from a child, and having to go without a lot of things in life, perhaps his idea was to try to become well off so that he could give us more, so that we had to put up with the inconvenience of a workshop in our home until he made good.

He made all manner of goods: wooden toys during the war, jewellery, trick playing cards, balloons, belts, soldiers, leather wallets, He dealt in receivers, empty wooden boxes, our living room being filled to capacity at one period. And after spending all his life trying, he finished with a few hundred pounds. He seemed to get his pleasure out of these activities, its true, but was it really worth it in respect of his family. If he had had the proper education and help, he could have achieved much more than he did.

So Dad went back to his flat in Tottenham, and during this time we had been given the offer of another place, for Jackman Street was due for slum clearance. At first the G.L.C. tried to con us into accepting another slum in place of the one we intended to move from; this place was in Greenwood Road, Dalston and it was literally falling to bits. The second offer was in Tottenham, another dilapidated antiquity, and again we refused. With this we went to the Kings Cross head office in a temper to see the person responsible for offering us such health-destroying accommodation.

There was a young girl at the desk, and behind her was a partition.

'I would like to speak to someone in charge, with a bit of authority round here,' I said.

'Well,' she said, 'I represent the G.L.C.'

I thought, this young girl of eighteen is here to listen to my housing problems, a girl not even married. How can such a youngster, no matter how good her intentions, understand the struggles of people trying simply to get a place to live? We explained our case.

'Well,' she said, 'we haven't anything else.'

I could not help feeling that the real person I should have been talking to was listening behind the partition, so I thought I would explain my case for the benefit of the hidden listener. This is how it went:

'You have offered us housing that could not be described as anything else but derelict. Does your chairman of the G.L.C. live in this sort of housing do you think? I am sure he doesn't. He probably lives in a house in Hampstead or something like that. He should then understand that other people want to live in nice housing as well. To offer this sort of thing to honest working class people is the worst sort of insult to put up with. When we got married we accepted this rubbish, because we had nothing else, but now we are a little older and wiser it isn't going to work this time. Thanks to your housing, as a child I contracted asthma. I simply refuse to have my condition aggravated even more by accepting the rotten housing you are offering me. I tell you, you will not get me out of Jackman Street until you give me something decent. You will not move me even if it means barricading myself in. Finally, do not insult me on your next offer; offer me a place fit for human habitation and I will willingly accept. Good day!'

And that was it – and it paid off, for we got a three bedroom flat, six years old, clean and roomy with plenty of light and air, a bath and an inside toilet. We were well pleased. It just shows that for people to get anything under this present system of things, they've got to assert themselves first. If you are afraid to complain, then you stay as you are.

I still used to go down to Tottenham to see Dad and take his paraffin for his oil fire. Although his new flat had central heating, he was unable to use it because it would have worked out too expensive on the money he was receiving on the labour. Sometimes I would leave it for about two weeks before going down there, and he would swear that it was a month. I knew how lonely he must have been on his own, but I knew at the same time that he would not come back with us.

By this time Dad had got his new dog, Sally; she was about nine months old when he got her. When I first saw her she reminded me of Trixie. I thought to myself, well he had Trixie for a long time, about fourteen years, and a thought came to my mind, I wonder if this dog will see Dad out, whether Dad will see another fourteen years. It is strange why I should have thought this, for Dad only lasted about three months after getting Sally.

It was one evening in July, 1973. I had just got home at six o'clock. As I got out my cab, Doll was standing at the door, tears streaming down her face. She waved to me to hurry up and I was taken with panic, wondering what was up. I thought, pull yourself together, panicking will only make whatever it is worse. As I came to the door:

'Dad's died,' she sobbed. I was stunned, as though stepping back on a scaffold, and realising too late your mistake. The reality of her words was too much. I just couldn't accept that he was gone.

So on the Monday was the funeral. The memories of childhood came flooding back. The time when I got beaten up in the street and he decided it was time for me to learn how to box. He would offer me sixpence if I made his nose bleed, a thing I succeeded in doing more than once, and feeling proud of myself, not realising that my father's nose bled easily. After being coached by my father for a few weeks he said,

'Right, now go out there and give it to 'em.'

Which I did willingly, eager to try out my new knowledge of self-defence.

There was a certain ducking technique he taught me that I will never forget, which got me out of trouble many a time. It was this technique that got me the championship of Darville Road. Roy Brown was a rather sturdily-built sort of boy, and it was he who had made mincemeat of me previously. He always used to like offering me a fight for some reason. I would always accept, for the sake of my image amongst the boys: it was bad enough getting a hiding, but to be a coward was even worse. I was always a small, weak sort of child, so perhaps I tried to make up for my physical weakness with my character. But now I was ready for the battle.

Along came Browning with the gang. I joined them, hoping all the time that he would ask me for a fight. At other times I would have dreaded it, but now I felt confident that I was skilled enough to take him on.

'All right, Barnsie, wanna fight then?'

'Well, er, er, do you really awnt to, then?'

70

Immediately the boys roared, 'Coward! Coward!'

'Well all right, then. we'll have a go.'

Then the boys made a circle leaning on each other leaving Brown and me in the middle, everyone looking tense and delighted, except Poshit, at the spectacle they were about to see. Brown came towards me, his fists as big as a leg of pork. I was on the retreat going round and round. Suddenly he swung me a right which caught the top of my head and sent me spinning. Then another left which smashed into my left rib and put me off balance. I tried to pull myself round, my head spinning. I thought, now keep your head and remember what your Dad told you. I kept my eye on Brown. Now then, I thought, Dad told me if your opponent is tall, go for his guts. Right, now this is where the ducking part comes in. So I crouched well down, feinted to the left, and moved in, only to come head on to an upper cut. My mouth was now dripping blood and I was almost ready to give up in defeat, but Brown had no idea what I was trying to do, for he was a fighter not a boxer. I must try it again, but time it better this time. So around we went again. I did my ducking as I had been trained. The two big fists came towards me. I moved my head to the left, ducked, and stepped to the right, my right fist burning itself deep into his left side. He let out a scream and down he went. He lay there doubled over, rocking back and forth, mouth open. I had floored him with one blow.

That was the last fight he had with me, and the boys respected me after that, small as I was.

'Blimey, Barnsie, that was a real Zattser that was. A crafty old duck as well. That was bleeding lovely that was, bleeding lovely.'

For this victory I had only my father to thank; without his help I never would have done it.

I remember the ghost stories he would tell his young brother and myself, frightening the wits out of us until we had to tell him to stop, but then so interesting did he made them that we had to keep on at him until we finished. He would always amuse kids, as well as myself, with tricks that would leave us dumbfounded. Yes, he could amuse children for hours and get as much, if not more, enjoyment from it as they did. His patience was unending.

71

Some time after these events I wrote a poem in memory of my father, it gives some idea of my picture of him.

*Dear dad you have departed so suddenly from us*
*We had no time to tell you*
*Just what you meant to us*

*We know you knew we loved you*
*But even just the same*
*We'd give the world to tell you*
*That we love you once again*

*We never will forget you Dad*
*The way you helped us out*
*The way you'd joke and cheer us up*
*Dispelling fear and doubt*

*You'd argue and you'd quarrel*
*And we'd say Ho whats the fuss*
*But little did we realise*
*It was your concern for us*

*I won't forget the times Dear Dad*
*We'd sit around and sing*
*And Brother D would give a prayer*
*Yes we had everything*

*On Sunday morn away you'd go*
*For that was market day*
*You'd then return with an old antique*
*What a bargain you would say*

*The kids around they loved you so*
*To them you were the tops*
*They called you by that sweet old name*
*That homely name of Pop.*

*With Trixie you would take your stroll*
*Just like you always did*
*They'd hold your hand*
*Or grasp your sleeve*
*Those ever present kids*

*When Bill Street came to see us*
*He would tap you for a fag*
*But the size you used to make them*
*Poor old Bill had just one drag*

*We won't forget that quiet voice*
*And the greying of your hair*
*The way you used to read and smoke*
*In that broken old armchair*

*And now you have departed*
*We find it hard its true*
*But one thing we are sure Dear Dad*
*Some day we'll be with you*

*And so we carry one life's road*
*And face life without fear*
*With this assurance deep inside*
*Our Dad is very near.*

I also wrote another poem.

*They are the disinherited*
*The ones that loved the most*
*Silently they bear the pain*
*No tears can flow to still the pain*

*They are the disinherited*
*No words no songs can tell*
*Their story*
*Words that seem to say you've been no son*
*Only the movement of a pen than it's done*

*They are the disinherited*
*Seeked favour found rejection*
*No more will this be*
*The final word is penned by thee*

*They are the disinherited*
*In sorrow they ask why*
*Not for wealth they might have lost*
*The price of love what is the cost?*

*They are the disinherited*
*Who when told did not believe*
*But then they saw the words so cold so few*
*Twas then they understood that it was true.*

# 10

And this brings me up to September, 1973, my life so far. How
long have I left, how much time to fulfil all my desires and ambitions?
About another twenty-five years with luck. Well, that isn't as long
as it sounds. What a pity that life is so short. It seems that just as
you begin to learn how to cope with life's problems it is almost
ended. What a pity that most of our time has to be spent earning a
living, and so little time spent on learning how to live it.

Have I had a hard life? No I don't think I have, compared to
many others. What are my feelings about the East End? Love and
hate I should say. The drab housing, the place where you work, the
coarseness of some of the people — but what can you expect with
people that have lived a hard life. Most people in the East End are
decent, hard-working people, and I emphasise that they work hard.

If I was asked the question, would I like my life over again, my
reply would be no. Then comes the question, why? I am not terribly
in love with this world. Just read the local papers with their court
cases, and the national papers with their reports of Vietnam, the
Middle East, and so on: in these papers you will read about the
plight of the human race.

I do not consider my childhood a happy one, although it wasn't
all that bad compared with working class standards of the time,
during the thirties and forties. Then there was my teenage life of
ignorance and uneventfulness and a harder life of poverty after
getting married. No, I don't think I would like that all over agian.

But now I can consider myself well off, now that I am a taxi-
driver and can work regularly, and make my money up if I do
become sick. Due to the lessening of anxiety over this problem, my
health has improved a great deal. Being a taxi-driver has opened my
eyes even more. You drive the well-heeled about all day, within the
West End, and on your way home, it might be raining, an old or
disabled East Ender waits at a bus stop and does not wave you
down. Reason: no money. You don't offer them a free lift because

they may get suspicous. You drive on thinking of all the healthy young beings you have been driving around all day, and having to pass those who need this type of transport most. If an old person in the East End does hail you, which is not very often, you charge them half fare. They don't argue, most of them can't see the clock anyway. But to give them a free ride would be an insult to them, so you have to charge them something.

These are the sort of things that I do not find very attractive about this life, and it seems that there is no changing it – it is all taken as the natural course of things, so acclimatised have we become to this state of affairs.

And yet althought here is poverty still, we are lucky in a way, especially when you hear things like my father used to tell me, like when he tried to make his own shoes because he couldn't afford to buy a pair. He was about eighteen at the time. He had watched a boot mender at work for some time, and saw how the shoes were put together. The boot mender had given him some scraps of leather and some advice on how to go about it. On finishing his shoes, which looked as though they were made by an expert, he was ready to go out. Dressed in his peeky cap, pink suit with bell bottoms away he went. By the time he had got to Bethnal Green Road from Poyser Street, the shoes had burst open like a pair of kippers. On seeing this shocking result of his shoddy workmanship, he imme-diately about turned and went flapping home as fast as he could go. How tragic and comical poverty can be.

Then there was the time when my father and uncle decided to decorate our flat so as to drive the bugs out for a while. In those days they used flour and water paste to put up wallpaper. They were at it all night so my mother and Aunt decided to go to bed. After Dad and Uncle had finished wallpapering, they woke us up and handed us some freshly cooked pancakes and tea. We got stuck into them – they were delicious. The next morning my mother remarked on them to Dad and Uncle about how she enjoyed them. My uncle and father were looking at each other with a knowing smile.

'Shall we tell 'em?' said my uncle.

My father nodded, still smiling.

'Well,' said my uncle. 'You know what we made them with, don't you?'

My mother looked a little worried at this.

'What?' she asked.

Then my uncle laughed,

'Out the bleeding wallpaper paste what we had over. Well, we were staiving after that job and there was nothing else. So that was it — pancakes.'

'Oh!' my mother shouted. 'You dirty pair of bleeders!'

She then told my Aunt Polly, and my Uncle George and father didn't hear the last of it for weeks. This must have happened when I was about five or six years old.

How much better things have become today. More opportunities for the young, better housing, the threat of unemployment lessened, the help of social security. But still there is room for improvement. People are still anxious about many things. Everything is by no means perfect and we must not rest complacent with what we have. Poverty, loneliness, homelessness are still with us, only not on so large a scale as in past years. Those of us living comfortably tend to forget those, who through no fault of their own, are suffering these things. And if we do forget them and are satisfied, then we should all be utterly ashamed, and not consider ourselves as human beings, and we should not rest until that time when all the sufferings of man are eliminated or eased to the utmost of our ability.

October 3 1973